GROWING CHINESE VEGETABLES
IN YOUR OWN BACKYARD

GROWING CHINESE VEGETABLES

IN YOUR OWN BACKYARD

Grow 40 Vegetables and Herbs in Gardens and Pots

Geri Harrington

Foreword by Norma Chang

Storey Publishing

IN LOVING MEMORY OF MY HUSBAND, DON HARRINGTON,
AND TO MY SONS, TY AND JEFF

*The mission of Storey Publishing is to serve our customers by
publishing practical information that encourages
personal independence in harmony with the environment.*

Edited by Gwen Steege and Elizabeth P. Stell
Art direction and page design by Jessica Armstrong
Front cover design and calligraphy by Alethea Morrison
Photography and illustration credits appear on page 216
Indexed by Nancy D. Wood

© 2009 by Jeff Harrington
Revised and updated from *Grow Your Own Chinese Vegetables*,
by Geri Harrington, Storey Publishing, © 1984

Printed in the United States by Versa Press
10 9 8 7 6 5 4 3 2 1

LIBRARY OF CONGRESS CATALOGING-IN-PUBLICATION DATA

Harrington, Geri.
  Growing Chinese vegetables in your own backyard / by Geri Harrington.
     p. cm.
  Includes index.
  ISBN 978-1-60342-140-9 (pbk. : alk. paper)
   1. Vegetables, Chinese. 2. Vegetable gardening. I. Title.
SB351.C54H37 2009
635—dc22
                                   2009001530

CONTENTS

PART ONE: THE CHINESE VEGETABLES

PART TWO: GROWING CHINESE VEGETABLES

FOREWORD

First published 30 years ago, Geri Harrington's *Grow Your Own Chinese Vegetables* is even more relevant today than it was then. In the intervening years, both gardeners and cooks have become increasingly curious about the cuisines of other cultures and increasingly confident in growing foods from the other side of the planet. North America been enriched by the growth of multiculturalism, and at home, the world seems much smaller. Travel has become easier and more common, and returning travelers are eager to eat at home the delicious foods that they discovered while abroad.

The Chinese have a rich and varied food culture, one that is also known to be extremely nutritious, and the fresher the ingredients, the more healthful the dishes will be. What could be fresher

than vegetables from your garden to your wok? Both experienced and novice gardeners will find the author's enthusiasm and out-of-the-box ideas refreshing, and all will discover, through her book, how these "Chinese" vegetables are as easy-to-grow as our more familiar "Western" vegetables.

In this book, you'll not only find complete information on the appearance and flavor of 40 Chinese vegetables and herbs, but also learn which ones are suitable for growing in your area, their cultural requirements, when to harvest them, and how to store them to maintain optimum quality. Equally important, you'll discover dozens of creative ways to prepare them and include them in your day-to-day menus, both Chinese and non-Chinese.

Happy Gardening! Happy Wokking!
— Norma Chang

ACKNOWLEDGMENTS

In a field such as this one, where there are, to my knowledge, no books in English that cover the subject comprehensively, I have had to rely to a large extent on the help of many individuals widely scattered throughout the United States. It would be impossible to list them all, although each piece of information — no matter how small — was a valuable contribution to the overall knowledge I was gradually able to accumulate and draw on in writing this book. The Department of Agriculture, through its research service, was especially helpful, as were the staff of the Brooklyn Botanic Garden and the New York Botanical Garden. I am indebted also to the Library of the Gray Herbarium of Harvard University.

The individuals I would like to single out for special thanks are: Shui-Min Block; Dr. Parker Hang, Yale University Press; Mrs. Parker Hang, East Asian Reading Room, Yale University; W. Bradford Johnson, Vegetable Crops Specialist, CES, Cook College, Rutgers University at New Brunswick; Donald M. Mohr, Monmouth County Senior Agent, CES, Rutgers University; Walter Pagels, San Diego, California; Jack Parsons, Extension Agent, CES, Oregon State University; William J. Sanok, Agricultural Program Leader, CES, Cornell University; Perry Slocum, President, Slocum Water Gardens; Pete Slocum, Slocum Water Gardens; Kent B. Tyler, Vegetable Specialist, CES, University of California at Parlier; Bill Uber, Van Ness Water Gardens; Professor Mas Yamaguichi, CES, University of California at Davis.

In addition, I would like to thank all the seed suppliers who were so generous with their time and advice that I was able to grow successfully even those vegetables with which I had no previous experience and to enjoy their new flavors and textures in my kitchen. I especially want to thank the people at the Kitazawa Seed Company for hunting up for me seeds that were not available in their catalog.

And — as always — my thanks to my husband, Don, who shared my interest in every new flower and fruit.

A PHOTO GUIDE TO THE
CHINESE VEGETABLES

MUSTARD GREENS, page 11

MUSTARD GREENS, page 11

GARLAND
CHRYSANTHEMUM, page 17

MIZUNA, page 14

VEGETABLE AMARANTH, page 6

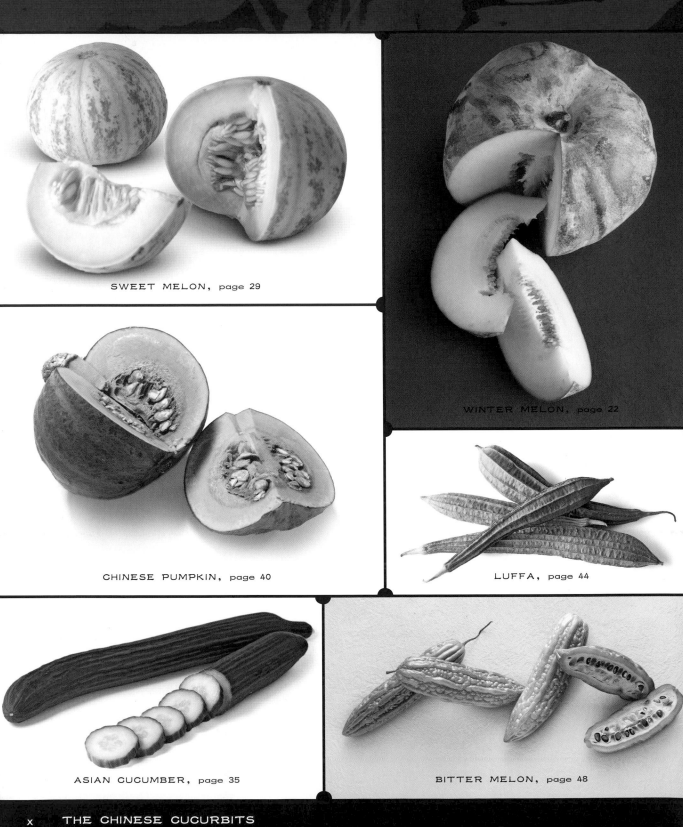

SWEET MELON, page 29

WINTER MELON, page 22

CHINESE PUMPKIN, page 40

LUFFA, page 44

ASIAN CUCUMBER, page 35

BITTER MELON, page 48

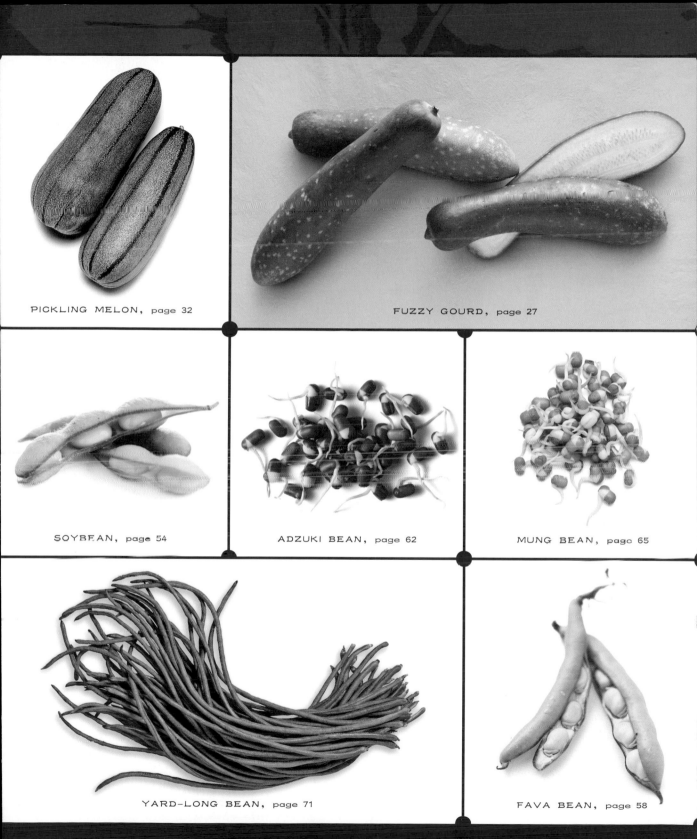

PICKLING MELON, page 32

FUZZY GOURD, page 27

SOYBEAN, page 54

ADZUKI BEAN, page 62

MUNG BEAN, page 65

YARD-LONG BEAN, page 71

FAVA BEAN, page 58

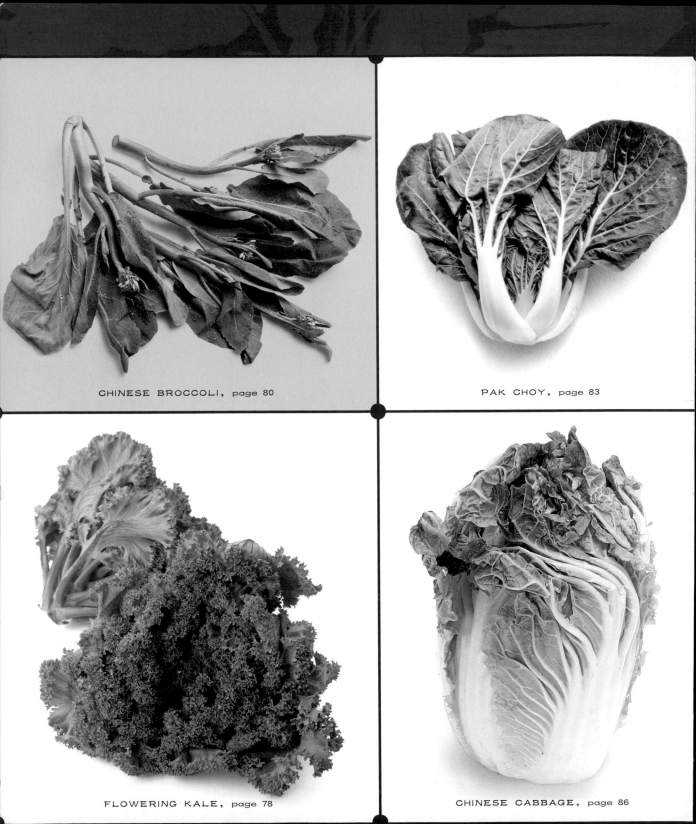

CHINESE BROCCOLI, page 80

PAK CHOY, page 83

FLOWERING KALE, page 78

CHINESE CABBAGE, page 86

CHINESE RADISH, page 105

BURDOCK, page 90

CHINESE EGGPLANT, page 110

SNOW PEA, page 98

DAYLILY, page 94

ASPARAGUS PEA, page 102

CILANTRO, page 128

GARLIC, page 117

GINGER, page 144

MITSUBA, page 132

GARLIC CHIVES, page 120

WATERCRESS, page 135

HOT PEPPER, page 124

SESAME (PLANT AND SEEDS), page 139

BUNCHING ONION, page 114

CHINESE LOTUS, page 162

VIOLET-STEMMED TARO, page 156

ARROWHEAD, page 167

WATER CHESTNUT, page 159

A TASTE OF CHINA

Americans used to be considered somewhat insular by the rest of the world — and, in a way, we were. As more and more of us traveled widely, however, the foods of the world no longer seemed that foreign and, inevitably, as we became interested in the food of other countries, we wanted to be able to cook and eat truly *authentic* dishes. The more I ate and cooked Asian food, the more I realized I would have to grow my own Chinese vegetables if I wanted to taste the real thing. Even going to Chinese restaurants became unsatisfactory; most limited themselves to a few authentic Chinese vegetables — snow peas, pak choy, bamboo shoots — and sometimes these were canned. If you're fortunate, you may live near an Asian grocery or farmer's market that sells fresh Chinese vegetables in season, but you may prefer to grow your own.

When I first considered growing Chinese vegetables in my own garden, I couldn't find books to tell me what the vegetables were or how to obtain seeds, let alone how to grow them. But I started hunting up seed sources and soon had my own garden going. Since then, the situation has improved; more and more regular seed companies carry Asian vegetables and identify them as such.

Not the least of the problems I encountered writing this book was determining the correct Chinese or Asian name for each vegetable, and the correct English equivalent. I had not realized how different Cantonese is from Mandarin, and how much they in turn differ from other Chinese languages. Two Chinese friends would invariably give me two different names for the same vegetable; others could pronounce the name but would leave it to me to work out the spelling phonetically. There is also very little consistency in the English spelling among Chinese reference books, since transliterating a Chinese word to an English phonetic equivalent has often been an arbitrary decision on the part of a Chinese writer. I found that most of the various spellings could be resolved by pronouncing them aloud. For instance, "gai choy" and "kai choi," if spoken aloud, are quickly recognized as the same thing. This system works best with Cantonese; if a word seems almost unpronounceable, chances are — in my experience — it is Mandarin.

To complicate matters further, I discovered that there has also arisen a "language" known as California Chinese, a variation of Cantonese. Many of these vegetables are grown commercially in California, and I sometimes thought I had come upon a new vegetable when I had merely found the California Chinese name for one I already knew.

Botanical names are universal, regardless of the country in which the vegetable is best known. They should always be your final arbiter in identifying any plant. All the names appear in the index for easy cross-reference.

I hope you will have as much pleasure growing and eating these fascinating vegetables as I have had in introducing them to you. I would like to close with an old Chinese proverb: "To be happy for a week, get married; to be happy for a month, kill a pig; and to be happy for a lifetime, plant a garden."

— *Geri Harrington*
Wilton, Connecticut

PART ONE

THE CHINESE VEGETABLES

Many Chinese vegetables have slowly become an everyday part of our diet. They're not in any way limited to Chinese cooking; Chinese vegetables fit in comfortably with familiar American recipes and their use is practically unlimited. When you reflect that many of the "American" foods we take for granted — carrots, beets, apples, and many more — aren't native to this country, you realize that a foreign vegetable is just one we haven't yet incorporated into our daily menus.

Growing Chinese vegetables is no different from trying a new hybrid tomato or corn, though in most cases Chinese vegetables seem to be prettier. Snow peas are more attractive to grow than English peas; Asian squash are more handsome and more interesting than jack-o-lanterns. Another difference, especially important to container gardeners, is that Asian vegetables generally seem to be more prolific. Here again, snow peas are a perfect example. Growing Chinese vegetables means good nutrition as well as great fun.

1

THE CHINESE GREENS

VEGETABLE AMARANTH • MUSTARD GREENS •
MIZUNA • GARLAND CHRYSANTHEMUM

Generally speaking, "greens" means vegetable leaves that are eaten cooked as opposed to "leafy greens," such as lettuces, that are primarily eaten raw. The dividing line is purely arbitrary and not at all consistent. For example, spinach was once considered edible only when cooked, until some brave soul nibbled on a raw leaf and found it good. On the other hand, Belgian endive (normally a raw salad vegetable in the United States) is excellent braised, and escarole cooked in the Italian fashion with a little olive oil is almost better than raw.

Traditional "greens" in the United States include kale, collards, Swiss chard, dandelions, and mustard greens. In the old days, they were welcomed in the spring after a winter that was barren of fresh vegetables; they could be sown and harvested before almost any other crop. Their taste was usually slightly bitter, and this had a tonic effect on winter-weary appetites.

Now, vitamin-rich greens are available year round. In addition to old favorites, you can grow and enjoy the greens of Asia: amaranth, Chinese mustard, mizuna, and garland chrysanthemum. They are easy to grow and take up very little space. They thrive in both vegetable and flower gardens, are low in calories and worth their weight in nutrition, and are deliciously different from the more familiar greens.

Vegetable Amaranth

Xian Cai, Een Choy

Amaranthus tricolor (leaf), also *A. hypochondriacus* (seeds)
(color photo, page ix)

Amaranth is an ancient vegetable grown in many parts of the world. *Amaranthus tricolor also goes by the names Chinese spinach, edible amaranth, hiyu, and callaloo. It's better known in the United States as an ornamental plant than as a vegetable. With brilliantly colored leaves and bright clusters of small flowers that bloom for many months, it's showy enough for any flower bed. Perhaps you've been growing amaranth for years and never knew it was edible.*

Most catalogs in North America list amaranth, but the majority place it in the flower section. To make sure you get an *edible* variety, look for one called vegetable amaranth; not all varieties are suitable. Though not botanically related to spinach, it can be cooked the same way, and it's even more nutritious. It relishes hot weather, so it makes a good substitute for spinach in the heat of summer.

Its use as cooked greens is only a small part of the potential of this amazing plant. By far its greatest use worldwide is as a grain. It's prolific — much more so than wheat, for instance — and a mere square yard of garden can yield up to 2 pounds of seeds. Unlike wheat, the seeds are easy to gather and can be cooked whole or ground into flour.

Before the Europeans came on the scene, this was a favorite food of the Aztecs, who cultivated the prolific plant as their main grain crop. History records that 200,000 bushels were paid annually as tribute to Montezuma, and use of this seed in this hemisphere can be traced back thousands of years. The Spanish conquistadors, disturbed by its use in Aztec religious ceremonies, forbade the Indians to grow it, but its cultivation continued surreptitiously.

For some reason, amaranth has been used in religious ceremonies wherever it has been grown. The ancient Greeks considered it a symbol of immortality (hence its name, which means "unfading") and pronounced it sacred to Artemis. They believed it possessed exceptional healing qualities and frequently depicted it in decorations on tombs and temples. India, China, Japan, and Guatemala also have many legends about amaranth and used it in their own sacred rituals. The Eastern Star Chapter of North American Masons — the largest Masonic woman's organization in the United States — has an Order of the Amaranth. Sweden has an Amaranter Order of Knighthood, established in 1653 by Queen Christina, who obviously chose the name because of the legendary reputation of the amaranth plant.

Appearance

Amaranth varies greatly in the color of its foliage, leaf shape, and height. Sometimes known as Joseph's Coat for its brilliant coloring, it ranges from a rosy crimson to a bright red-and-green variegation. Leaves can vary so much in shape that you won't always recognize them as belonging to an amaranth.

The tiny flowers would be insignificant except they occur in such large numbers that the overall effect is outstanding. If growing amaranth for the leaves, you won't want to encourage the flowers or let the plants go to seed, but amaranth has such a long harvest season that you may reach a point where you welcome a few weeks without this leafy vegetable on the table. Then you can let the plants flower and go to seed. If you grow amaranth for its seeds, you'll naturally have a long season of beautiful flowers.

Most types grow 2 to 3 feet in height, although some reach considerably higher. Some of the lower-growing varieties tend to be somewhat straggling; others are very compact and bushy. All require good air circulation, so don't crowd them with other vegetables (or tall flowers, if you put them in the flower bed). If the plants get too tall, stake them with bamboo poles or tomato stakes. The seed varieties are usually erect and need no support.

How to Grow

Getting started. Amaranth is sensitive to frost and germinates best in warm soil. Wait to plant until after the last frost when the ground warms up, start indoors four weeks before the last frost, or follow the planting times recommended on the seed packet or in the seed catalog.

Planting. Generally speaking, sow seeds shallowly (no more than ¼ inch deep), ½ inch apart, in rows 18 inches apart. Check the seed packets for specific recommendations. Keep the seeds moist until the first set of true leaves appears.

Amaranth grows so quickly that only the most eager gardeners will start seeds indoors. (See page 201.) If you want an extra-early crop of amaranth, try a small sowing. Keep seeds and then seedlings moist, and keep an eye on the growth. Since amaranth can be fussy about transplanting, be even more careful than usual about disturbing the roots when transplanting. As soon as the soil has warmed up, harden off seedlings and set them out where they are to stay in your garden. Shade them if a hot spell coincides with this move. Keep the soil around them moist so that roots move into it with the least difficulty.

Growing needs. Amaranth grows freely in many climates, in warm or cold. It requires full sun but isn't fussy about anything else. Once seedlings are growing well, plants tolerate heat and drought and aren't much bothered by pests. Fertilize lightly; overfertilizing results in over-large, often tough leaves.

When seedlings are 2 inches high, thin plants to 2 inches apart. Pull up the entire plant you're thinning and enjoy these excellent baby greens. Cut off the roots and wash leaves in lukewarm water to remove soil. Then steam or stir-fry for 2 minutes. Continue to thin by harvesting every other plant until the plants are 10 to 18 inches apart (or

DID YOU KNOW?

Amaranth is not only versatile and delicious, it's also one of the most nutritious vegetables or grains you can eat. The leaves are rich in vitamins and minerals — even more than beet greens — and are easy to digest. The seeds are also good sources of vitamins, minerals, and fiber. Seeds contain more protein than common cereal grains. The protein is very high quality; it's considered a complete protein because it has a better balance of amino acids than soybeans, whole wheat, or milk. Amaranth seeds are also a good source of calcium and iron.

whatever final spacing is recommended on the seed packet).

How to Harvest

For greens. When plants are 6 to 8 inches tall, begin to harvest outer leaves. Plants mature in about 50 days for greens and 100 or more days for seeds. Cut the tops and youngest leaves to delay flowering and prolong harvest. If you want seeds, not greens, you can enjoy the flowers for a long time. In Connecticut they flower from July through September, slowing down when the weather turns cool.

For seeds. Wait until seeds are fully mature and almost dry. Pull up the entire plant, cut off the roots, and hang upside down in a warm dry place in a paper bag. Label the bags to keep the varieties separate; this is important both for taste tests and to identify the variety when you plant next year. When completely dry, shake the plants in the bags to allow seeds to fall to the bottom and be easily collected. Check plants for any seeds that remain and hand-pick.

Once the seeds are completely dry, store in airtight containers in a cool, dry place. Seeds can be cooked alone or mixed with cereal grains, or ground into flour. The flour contains no gluten and combines well with other flours in baked goods like biscuits and bread. Reserve some seeds for planting next year.

Remove the top few inches to delay flowering and prolong the harvest.

Varieties

Amaranthus tricolor has attractively variegated, edible green-and-red leaves. The same species is sometimes sold as *A. gangeticus*, Greek amaranth. *A. hypochondriacus* produces abundant seeds but is not the best variety for greens.

To get the most delicious varieties, look for vegetable amaranth, or ask to make sure the variety is edible as well as ornamental. Try different kinds each year until you find one you like best. Since amaranth is so ornamental, try several different kinds in one season by planting some in flower beds.

Varieties to look for: Red Stripe Leaf, Tender Leaf, All Red.

The flavor of amaranth greens is variously described as meaty, spinach with a pinch of horseradish, rather hot (or rather bland, depending on the variety), aromatic, or slightly sweet but tangy. Some of these apparent contradictions are due to the many varieties of vegetable amaranth, which vary in taste as well as in appearance. All have a unique flavor, unlike that of any other vegetable.

COOKED GREENS. Although occasionally used in salad mixes, amaranth is mostly eaten as cooked greens. It cooks in a few minutes and can be steamed, like spinach, just in the water left on it after washing. Large leaves can be coarsely chopped before cooking. A crushed clove of garlic added to the pot, and a dressing of Asian sesame oil tossed with the cooked leaves, makes a delectable vegetable.

HOT OR CHILLED SOUP. If allowed to cook more than 5 minutes, amaranth becomes mushy. Take advantage of this fact and simmer it longer in chicken broth. When it becomes thoroughly limp, purée the leaves with some of the broth in the blender and add cream or yogurt, a bit of curry, a pinch of turmeric, and perhaps a little salt. Reheat in the pot of broth without boiling. Stir to blend thoroughly and serve as an unusual hot or chilled soup. A garnish of crisp, thinly sliced water chestnuts makes a good finishing touch.

OTHER USES. In China and Japan, amaranth is widely used in soups and stir-fry dishes, or steamed as a side dish. It combines well with garlic, ginger, grated radish, scallions, pork, soy sauce, lemon, and sake to make a delicious main dish. Wherever your Chinese cookbook calls for spinach, use amaranth. It is a popular ingredient in buffets throughout the East Indies. In the West Indies, it is cooked with rice, tomatoes, and ham, and simmered until the rice is tender.

The high protein content of amaranth seed makes it a welcome addition to diets throughout the world, and a boon to vegetarians. The flour can be added to breads, cakes, sauces, soups, stews, and many other dishes.

Mustard Greens

Jie Cai, Gai Choy

Brassica juncea
(color photos, page ix)

If the only mustard greens you've ever eaten are the common garden variety, you may be inclined to turn away from this vegetable without another thought. The mustard greens commonly available in North America are too pungent for many tastes. Chinese mustard greens, or Chinese mustard, are not: they are among the most delicious of all greens.

Chinese mustard is a native of Asia, where it has been under cultivation for thousands of years. A close relative of the common mustards, its taste is quite different — as one person in a family may be peppery in temperament while another is only mildly so. Some varieties are described as tasting like Dijon mustard when eaten raw. Chinese mustard isn't usually found in the produce section, unless you live near a Chinese market, so you must grow your own to enjoy it. You may find it called Indian mustard or takana.

Appearance

Chinese mustard comes in many forms, like leaf lettuces. The leaves may be broad and flat, curled, crinkled, or feathery. Plants can grow from 12 to 18 inches in height. Since the flavor of one will vary slightly from another, try several — easy to do in a single season, since this fast-growing crop lends itself to successive sowings.

The seeds are small, round, and dark red to almost black. In India and Asia they are pressed for their oil, which has medicinal as well as culinary uses.

How to Grow

Getting started. Sow in early spring, as soon as the ground can be worked, and again from early August until the first frost. Most varieties do not do well in midsummer. In hot weather, the flavor becomes peppery strong, and plants bolt (flower). If you want to enjoy it all summer long, seek out varieties described as slow to bolt, keep seedlings well watered, and harvest leaves when they're still young.

Planting. Sow the small seeds ¾ inch apart, in rows 12 to 18 inches apart, and cover with a ¼ inch of soil. When seedlings are 2 to 3 inches tall, thin to stand 2 inches apart. If you plan to harvest greens at full size (12 to 18 inches tall), continue thinning until plants are 10 inches apart to allow clumps to develop.

Growing needs. Chinese mustard tastes best when it's kept growing briskly. Keep well watered and fertilize weekly with half-strength liquid fertilizer or fish emulsion. Weeding and mulching helps to conserve moisture.

How to Harvest

Maturity dates range from 35 to 50 days, depending on the variety. Don't wait this long, though. Harvest from the time the plants are 3 inches tall. For salad greens, stop harvesting once plants exceed 8 inches in height. Taller than that, the leaves become very pungent, more like common mustard. Rather than treating them as cut-and-come-again salad greens, it's better to pull up plants and start a new crop.

Varieties

You've probably encountered a red form of Chinese mustard in mesclun salad mixes, as it's a popular ingredient for its color and Dijon mustard flavor.

DID YOU KNOW?

Either raw or cooked, Chinese mustard is a rich source of many vitamins and minerals, especially vitamins A, B$_6$, C, riboflavin, and iron. For that reason, it has been considered useful as a spring tonic.

Chinese mustard comes in two forms, *Brassica juncea* ssp. *rugosa* and *B. juncea* ssp. *foliosa*. In appearance they differ primarily in the color of the foliage. The *rugosa* has brownish red leaves, while the *foliosa* has dark-green leaves.

The *rugosa* has broader, thicker stems (like Swiss chard) that can be used separately from the leaves and cooked like asparagus.

Varieties to look for: Bau-Sin, San-Ho Giant, Red Giant.

— CULINARY USES —

SALAD. You can combine Chinese mustard in salads with other greens, or make a small salad of just this attractive green as a zesty side dish, garnished with minced hard-boiled egg and tossed in vinaigrette made with a dash of lemon juice (but no mustard).

COOKED GREENS. In cooking, treat it just like spinach. Steam briefly over a very small quantity of boiling water (longer cooking makes it less flavorful) and toss with Asian sesame oil and soy sauce. Use it instead of spinach in your favorite quiche recipe, or combine with a cream sauce for delicious crêpes. It also makes an interesting green sauce for pasta, whirled in a blender with melted butter and a couple of garlic cloves and briefly heated. Try them cooked Southern-style with a bit of lemon, a dash of vinegar, and some bacon bits.

USING THE STEMS. Prepare the broader, thicker stems of some varieties separately, cooked like asparagus. In Asia, the stems are very popular in stir-fry dishes and are frequently pickled. To pickle, save the liquid from your next batch of pickles (your own or commercial ones), heat to the boiling point, cool to lukewarm, and pour over the cut-up stems. Refrigerate for three or four days and serve. Be sure the liquid isn't too warm when you pour it over the stems or you'll sacrifice the crunchiness of a good pickle.

OTHER USES. Chinese mustard adds character to clear soup and makes an excellent vegetable to stir-fry with ginger, pak choy, bean sprouts, snow peas, and mushrooms. For a heartier version, add a bit of shredded chicken or pork.

Mizuna

Ri Ben Shue Cai

Brassica napa nipposinica
(color photo, page ix)

This Asian green is sometimes called Chinese potherb mustard or Japanese salad green. In California, you may occasionally encounter it under the name California peppergrass, but this is a misnomer since it's not related to peppergrass and is not at all peppery. Although a member of the Mustard family, it lacks the pungency of either the common or Chinese mustards.

Appearance

Like so many Asian vegetables, mizuna is worthy of being grown purely as a decorative plant. When not in flower, its feathery, light green leaves form an ornamental clump up to 12 inches in diameter — compact and upright. Use it as a graceful bedding plant, a delicate foliage accent, or a beautiful background for low-growing ageratum or alyssum.

It's particularly useful for filling that awkward period in the flower garden, when the spring crocuses and daffodils must still be accommodated, even though they're no longer an asset. Mizuna grows quickly and high enough to hide fading daffodil foliage. When you harvest mizuna for the kitchen, you can fill the spot in the flower bed with warm-weather annuals.

How to Grow

Getting started. Though it looks delicate, mizuna is ideal as an early spring green, cold hardy and tolerant of wet soil. In Connecticut, where springs are so often chilly and wet, it compensates for failures due to the too early, over-enthusiastic sowing of other seeds that can't possibly germinate under these adverse conditions. If your green beans are rotting in the ground, it's comforting to see a fine row of mizuna seedlings well on their way.

Grow mizuna successively from early spring on, until stopped by a hard frost. Continue sowing even after midsummer. Sometimes mizuna will survive the first snowfall and give you greens to gather well after the rest of the garden has given up for the season. I've actually had mizuna green and fresh after a frost that destroyed my zinnias.

In spite of being comfortable with cold weather, mizuna — unlike lettuce — won't go to seed in a spell of hot weather. I have grown it through a week of 90°F temperatures without any ill effect except slight wilting, and that corrected itself when the temperatures cooled off in the evening.

Planting. Sow seeds 2 inches apart, about ½ inch deep and in rows 18 inches apart. Once the plants begin to crowd one another, start thinning; these young thinnings are delicately delicious. For plants to grow to full size, keep thinning until they are about 12 inches apart. For use as a bedding plant, thin to 10 inches apart.

Growing needs. Frequent watering and applications of diluted liquid fertilizer or fish emulsion starting three weeks after germination are all the attention this vegetable needs. It seems remarkably free from pests and diseases.

For successive sowings, prepare the soil before seeding by digging in some compost and fertilizer to replenish that used up by the previous crop. Don't overdo the fertilizer; growth should be brisk but not headlong.

How to Harvest

Take a few leaves from each plant anytime starting three weeks after germination. The major harvest should be completed in 35 to 40 days. You can take the whole plant or just most of the leaves. Mizuna works well for cut-and-come-again harvesting, perfect for salad mixes. Clip the entire row to within an inch of their bases after four to five weeks for baby greens. If you fertilize as if you were reseeding, plants will regrow quickly for a second cutting. This is easier than reseeding or transplanting seedlings, and a tremendous timesaver.

I generally prefer to harvest the entire plant, and replant with seedlings that have been started elsewhere. I am constantly changing my garden plan and often want to put a plant in quite a different spot. It's very easy to have a flat of mizuna seedlings ready for transplanting. Or, drop in a seed whenever you harvest a whole plant, and you'll have a rest between harvests. What with lettuces, chards, mustards, cabbages, and other leafy vegetables, I must admit that sometimes they get away from me, but I've discovered this happens to all enthusiastic gardeners — *all* of us plant too much zucchini, for instance.

Clip the entire plant to within an inch of its base for baby greens; it will regrow quickly for a second cutting.

Varieties

Several varieties are now available, including some with reddish tints. If you don't find it listed under mizuna, try looking under gourmet greens, Asian greens, mustard greens, or salad mixes.

Varieties to look for: Mizuna Mustard, Organic Mizuna Early, Japanese Green.

- CULINARY USES -

Rich in vitamins and minerals, mizuna is so mildly flavored that it's hard to believe it's a close relative of mustard greens. Its feathery foliage is very attractive in a leafy tossed salad of mixed greens. If mixed with other mild salad greens, a bit of mustard in the vinaigrette dressing would be nice.

When the weather is cool, and hot food more welcome, try any of the following:

• Combine it (at the last minute) with a steaming dish of turnips and carrots.

• Stir-fry in sesame oil with ginger and soy sauce for flavoring.

• Use in clear soups or as a last-minute addition to minestrone. It makes an unusually fine cream soup, garnished with a sprinkling of garlic chives.

Garland Chrysanthemum

Tong Hao Cai, Tong Ho

Chrysanthemum coronarium

(color photo, page ix)

If you grow many of the wonderful Chinese vegetables in this book, your neighbors will be very confused; they won't be able to tell your vegetable garden from your flower garden. Also known as shungiku or edible chrysanthemum, this plant is a true chrysanthemum, with recognizable chrysanthemum flowers. Only you will know that it's also a superb vegetable. (Don't rush to nibble at your flower-bed chrysanthemums, however; you'll find them much too bitter.)

Garland chrysanthemum is a native of the lands around the Mediterranean, where it's known as crown daisy. The Asian countries have taken it as their own, along with all other chrysanthemums. In China, the chrysanthemum is a symbol of a life of ease and joviality and is appreciated by the over-30 adults as the symbol of late-blooming beauty. In Japan, it's the national flower and is used as a stylized decorative element in Japanese art and architecture. The high regard in which it's held is also shown by the fact that it is used in one of the dishes served as part of the Japanese tea ceremony.

Appearance

Garland chrysanthemum grows from 2 to 4 feet high. Foliage is dark green, pleasantly aromatic, and very attractive. The daisylike flowers vary in color from white to yellow to orange. Usually garland chrysanthemum is eaten as a green long before it has had a chance to flower. Always let a few plants flower, however; the blooms are pretty and they're fun to eat. Like all chrysanthemums, this vegetable is long-flowering and will bloom in your garden from August until killed by hard frost. Plant between rows of ruby chard and you'll find yourself out in the vegetable garden with a camera.

How to Grow

Getting started. Plant garland chrysanthemum early in spring, as soon as the ground can be worked, and sow successively until early summer. If grown during hot weather, it becomes slightly bitter, but you can plant it again in late summer for a fall crop.

Planting. Sow the small seeds thinly, if possible, ¼ to ½ inch deep, about 2 inches apart and in rows 18 inches apart. Start thinning as soon as plants reach a couple of inches tall. Young leaves, gathered while the plant is still immature, make the best eating.

Growing needs. Like most vegetables, garland chrysanthemum likes a rich, humusy soil. Keep the plants well weeded and watered — mulch is a big timesaver — and they'll thrive without any other particular care. If you incorporated fertilizer before sowing, they won't need further feeding. The plants tolerate partial shade, so save your sunniest spots for more demanding vegetables.

How to Harvest

Gather leaves when plants are no more than 4 to 6 inches tall. Spring-sown plants can be gathered, plant by plant, as wanted. If you want flowers, harvest seedlings in such a way as to thin out the row, leaving room for plants to fill out. They generally bloom about 60 days from seed. The flowers make quite a show in the vegetable garden.

Varieties

There are at least two varieties: one small with medium-lobed ("fine") leaves and a somewhat taller one with deeply serrated leaves. The florists' chrysanthemum (a different species, *Chrysanthemum × morifolium*) is frequently used in Japan for making dried flower petals.

Varieties to look for: Small Leaf, Round Leaf, Tiger Ear.

You can eat garland chrysanthemum raw with other salad greens, but more commonly, it's cooked. Be sure to cook *very briefly,* in a small amount of water, like spinach. This green tastes exactly the way chrysanthemums smell. When you first try it, combine it with other greens or vegetables until you see if you like it. Coarsely chopped and added to chicken broth with a thin slice of fresh ginger, it produces a soup that is an instant trip to China.

STIR-FRY. Stir-fry dishes make good use of this "fragrant green," as it's sometimes called. Combine it with bamboo shoots, snow peas, and bean sprouts for a rich variety of texture and taste that is truly Asian. Serve it as a side dish with a little Asian sesame oil, soy sauce, and a dash of sherry, along with pork or chicken. Or be completely Chinese and shred the pork or chicken directly into the same skillet. Cook it with spinach, beet greens, or Swiss chard to create a vegetable melange, but don't confuse the palate by combining it with any of the mustards.

JAPANESE-STYLE. You might try the Japanese custom of dipping the flowers in slightly warm sake at the beginning of a meal. This is said to confer good health and long life on the diner. (You may want to dip the flowers in boiling, salted water before serving them.) If you don't have sake, a medium-dry sherry will do almost as well.

DRIED FLOWER PETALS. Use these in soups, stir-fry dishes, and tempura. They should be soaked in tepid water before adding to the pot.

JAPANESE PICKLE. A very fragrant Japanese pickle, kikumi, is made with fresh chrysanthemum petals. Gather the flowers, remove the green base, and separate the petals. Drop in boiling, salted water and drain at once. Pat dry with paper towels. Marinate for an hour in sake and soy sauce. To be completely authentic, the marinade should also include chopped, pickled peaches or apricots. The pickle keeps in the refrigerator for several days.

HOW TO DRY CHRYSANTHEMUM FLOWERS

To dry garland chrysanthemum or other chrysanthemum flowers for culinary use, gather when they have fully opened. Remove the green base and separate the petals. Dip the petals in boiling, salted water, remove at once; and dry on a paper towel. Spread the petals in a single layer on a flat surface and dry in the sun (or in a 150°F oven) before storing.

In Japan only yellow flowers are used, but this seems to be an aesthetic consideration rather than a culinary one. There is no discernible difference in flavor from other color flowers.

2

THE CHINESE CUCURBITS

WINTER MELON • FUZZY GOURD • SWEET MELON
• PICKLING MELON • ASIAN CUCUMBER • CHINESE
PUMPKIN • LUFFA • BITTER MELON

Often called cucurbits, the Cucumber family (*Cucurbitaceae*) is a large group that includes all melons, all gourds, pumpkins, cucumbers, and squashes. These plants tend to take up a great deal of room in the garden; the majority are vines. All are subject to the same pests and diseases, and most like the same growing conditions. A few cucurbit plants will attract many pollinating bees, which feed heavily on the mostly orange or yellow blossoms.

In this chapter you'll find many unusual, fun things to grow that are also good eating. Even the Asian cucumbers are very different from our own — especially their extraordinary shapes. The serpent cucumber, for instance, can curl around in a circle with its "head" raised as if to see what you're up to.

Even if you're told that melons "don't do well" in your area, try them: I was warned off cantaloupes in Connecticut, but when I finally planted some anyhow, I had a huge crop of cantaloupes that spoiled store-bought ones for me forever. Conditions in garden sites vary so much that you may have luck with a vegetable your neighbor can't grow at all. The only way to tell is to try for a couple of seasons.

Winter Melon

DONG GUA, TUNG KWA
Benincasa hispida
(color photo, page x)

There's a very good chance that you've never seen, let alone eaten, a Chinese winter melon, even if you often eat in Chinese restaurants. In China and Japan, however, it is a staple, widely grown and used in almost every kind of dish.

Unlike some Chinese vegetables, this one has many names. Commonly called white or wax gourd because of its appearance, it is also known as ash melon for the same reason. Because it makes a delicious pickle, it is sometimes called Chinese preserving melon. Latin American markets may carry it under the name *calabaza China*.

All parts of the winter melon vine can be eaten — young leaves and flower buds as well as immature and mature fruits. The somewhat bitter seeds are an acquired taste, but it's worth toasting a batch to see how you like them.

Grow a few vines just for fun. It's very decorative in the garden and sensational in the kitchen. You can use it in everyday dishes ranging from soup to relish tray to main vegetable, limited only by your own imaginative approach to cooking. Most amazing is its keeping quality. Properly stored, it will stay fresh for a whole year.

Appearance

Winter melon grows on a *single*, somewhat hairy vine, rather than the branched vines of other melons. It's easy to train on a fence or other support, where it takes up much less room than on the ground (and also helps prevent rotting).

The melon itself is very large. It may reach 12 inches long and 8 inches wide at maturity and weigh as much as 25 pounds. Oblong or round in shape, it starts out a pretty green that gradually becomes coated with a white waxy substance as it matures. The flesh is white and looks something like a honeydew, although it tastes more like a slightly sweet zucchini, if you can imagine that.

How to Grow

Getting started. Winter melon is a warm-weather crop and (like most melons) requires a long growing season, about 150 days. If you won't have enough warm weather before the fall frosts, start the seeds indoors. Set out as soon as the ground has warmed up and all danger of frost is past. If you grow watermelon, set out winter melon at about the same time, or a little earlier.

Planting. If sown outdoors, plant seeds 1 inch deep and 8 to 10 inches apart. Like bitter melon, winter melon requires rich, fertilized soil to grow well. One way to assure a good crop is to dig a trench 8 to 10 inches deep and fill it with 4 inches of a high-nitrogen fertilizer mixed with compost or well-rotted manure. Mix the remaining soil with the same compost-fertilizer blend and fill in the trench. Then sow the seeds. Water thoroughly and keep watered until seedlings appear.

Growing needs. Moisture is essential for good fruit production; keep ground moist at all times. Water weekly — even more often in dry weather. If you don't have too many vines, try sinking a coffee can with holes punched all around the sides and the bottom removed in the ground between each vine. Fill this can with water several times when you do your regular watering; the results will amaze you.

Make a slow-dripping, self-watering can by punching holes in a coffee can, filling it with water, and sinking it into the ground next to each vine.

If you added fertilizer before planting as suggested, side-dressing isn't essential, but it's still a good idea. Side-dress (or water with fish-and-seaweed fertilizer) when the flowers appear and every two weeks thereafter.

Frequent watering means the soil will be moist a good deal of the time. This can cause fruits to rot from resting on the ground. Mulch with hay or straw or similar dry mulch material for the fruits to rest on, or elevate individual fruits on small, empty plastic tubs or coffee cans.

If you want to grow the vine up a support, be sure the support is sturdy enough to hold the large fruits. The legs of old panty hose or strips of nylon bird netting make good slings when the fruits get too heavy for the vine and need to be supported (see illustration on page 30).

How to Harvest

Young leaves and flower buds can be harvested whenever they appear. Immature melons can be cut from the vines as you want them. Mature melons are unmistakable: they are covered with a heavy white waxy coating when fully ripe. Use clippers to cut them from the vine, leaving some stem attached to the fruit.

Varieties

Several varieties of winter melon are now available.

Varieties to look for: Hybrid Wonder Wax, Round Tong Gwa, Hybrid Small Round.

STORING WINTER MELONS

Not the least of this extraordinary melon's virtues is its ability to keep for long periods. It may be stored for six months to a year if you have the right place for it. So long as the rind is not broken, the flesh will stay sweet and fresh for many, many months. The storage area should be cool (but not less than 50°F) and dry. Keep the melon in the position in which it was growing; this is the way it should be put on the shelf.

For short-term storage, a warm place — even an out-of-the-way spot in your pantry — will work as long as it's dry. Once you cut into a melon, store the rest in the refrigerator; it will keep for about a week.

There are many easy ways to use winter melon:

- It's good stir-fried with pork, scallions, and mizuna.

- The immature fruits are delicious in seafood curries.

- If you want an interesting pickle, prepare the rind like watermelon pickle.

CARVED MELON BOWL. The most famous dish is rather elaborate. Both the preparation and presentation of this dish make it suitable only for a banquet or a very special occasion. You could stake your entire culinary reputation on this one dish. For this dish, the melon must be completely ripe, covered with a heavy, waxy, white coating. Scrub off the waxy coating with a stiff brush to reveal the beautiful celadon green skin underneath, then follow these steps:

1. Carve the skin, like a cameo, into a bas-relief dragon or other suitable design. (In China these are sometimes amazingly detailed and elaborate.) The result can look like a rare Chinese bowl. If you aren't up to this, even simple geometric designs are attractive. The green outside and creamy underskin make it easy to create a work of art.

2. Cut off the top with a saw-toothed edge, like a jack-o'-lantern, and reserve. Remove seeds and fibers.

3. Find a pot that will hold the whole melon. Since a mature winter melon may be 12 inches long and 8 inches thick, this needs a large pot. If your pot is wide enough but not quite deep enough, cover with foil to keep in the steam.

4. Place the melon in the pot, suspended in the following manner: Make a sling out of a several thicknesses of cheesecloth, since the melon is so large and will become a little soft when cooked. This sling should go under the melon and hang

(continued on next page)

out of the pot on both sides so you can grab the ends to lift the melon out of the pot when it is done. The melon will be very heavy because it will be filled with broth and vegetables, so make your sling sturdy and easy to manage. Use a rack or some other method to keep the melon above the boiling water so it steams rather than boils. If you use a colander with feet, you could make handles of wire instead of the sling described above.

5. Fill the melon with Chinese vegetables cut into ¼-inch chunks. These can include lotus root, bamboo shoots, mushrooms (whole button or sliced larger ones), water chestnuts, and so on. Raw chicken, raw pork, and baked ham, also cut in small pieces, are usually added. Pour hot chicken broth over the vegetables until the melon is three-quarters full. Dried tangerine peel that has been soaked in water for 30 minutes is usually added at this time and removed just before serving. (If you don't have this, stir in grated orange rind just before taking the melon out of the pot.)

6. Cover the filled melon with its top, then cover the pot. Steam for 3 or 4 hours, or until the inside of the melon is tender.

To serve, bring the whole melon to the table on a flat platter. Serve from the melon at the table, stirring to mix the ingredients each time. This dish is a bit of a fuss, but it's worth it both for flavor and appearance. It isn't something to make every Sunday, however.

SIMPLE SOUP. A simpler version of the same soup can be made by scrubbing, peeling, and seeding the melon, then cutting it up into small chunks. Simmer in chicken broth with the other vegetables until the melon is tender. It is just as good and much quicker — though not nearly so spectacular — as cooking the melon whole.

Fuzzy Gourd

Mao Gua, Tsit Gua

Benincasa hispida var. *chieh-gua*

(color photo, page xi)

If the size of winter melons intimidates you, the fuzzy gourd will be just right. Its culture and growth habit are similar to the winter melon. If you're especially fond of these Chinese melons, this will give you an earlier crop than the winter melon. It also goes by the names hairy melon, hairy gourd, and hairy cucumber.

Appearance

Fuzzy gourds are vaguely pear-shaped but without a waist. They taper top and bottom and are either plumply oval or round. The vines are single-stemmed and should be tied onto a pole, or in a straight line up a fence. The fruits are an attractive green with sweet white flesh.

How to Grow

Getting started. Fuzzy gourd is a warm-weather vegetable; wait to sow until all danger of frost has passed and the ground is warm. Like winter melon, this grows best in well-fertilized soil.

Planting. Set seeds 1 inch deep and 2 inches apart next to a fence, trellis, or pole. Be patient; it will be 10 to 14 days before the seeds germinate. Keep the soil moist until seedlings have their second set of true leaves. When the seedlings are 3 inches tall, thin to stand about 5 inches apart.

Growing needs. Fuzzy gourd *must* be staked and the fruits allowed to hang free from the vines. You won't need to provide slings or other supports for the fruits because they won't be that heavy.

Fuzzy gourd benefits from regular feeding. When the seedlings are 3 inches tall, fertilize lightly — half-strength fish emulsion is good once a week. When fruits begins to form, fertilize every two weeks. Provide plenty of moisture all through the growing season.

How to Harvest

Like all members of this family, fuzzy gourd should be harvested when young. Pick when gourds are 4 to 6 inches long, though you can let some mature to provide next year's seeds.

Varieties

The difference in varieties is mostly in shape rather than in taste, so it needn't concern you. You may not have much choice in any case.

Varieties to look for: Seven Star Long, Chiang Shin Joker, Fuzzy Star F1 Hybrid.

— CULINARY USES —

Like winter melon, fuzzy gourd is eaten as a vegetable rather than a fruit. It can be used in all the same ways as yellow summer squash and zucchini — for soup, bread, casseroles, stir-frying, and so on.

The outside has a distinctly fuzzy coat, like an especially fuzzy peach, which must be removed. Do not cut it open until you have done this. Rub the gourd with paper towels to take off the fuzz, then peel off the green skin.

BAKED STUFFED GOURD. Fuzzy gourd is a good size and a nice shape for stuffing, just big enough that each half makes a single portion. You can stuff it as the Chinese do with shrimp, pork, bamboo shoots, pak choy, and scallions all cut up and mixed with soy sauce, Asian sesame oil, ginger, and minced garlic. Or use your favorite zucchini recipe, which might include tomatoes, chopped beef, oregano, basil, garlic, olive oil, and minced onion (brown the beef lightly in the garlic and oil). The seeds and core can be chopped up and added to this, just as with zucchini.

Sweet Melon

Xiang Gua, Tian Gua

Cucumis melo

(color photo, page x)

The sweet Asian melons, or Oriental melons, are more like what you'd expect of a melon — similar to honeydews and cantaloupes but very superior melons. You'll find some of them much easier to grow than the common varieties. If you like to grow melons, don't miss these. Even if you've had difficulty with regular melons, give them a try.

Appearance

Asian melons look much the same as melons in the West, with somewhat the same variations in size and color of rind and flesh. Most varieties run 1 to 3 pounds in size, which makes them very convenient for a home garden — although they still take up more space than most crops.

How to Grow

Getting started. Like most melons, sweet Asian melons require unvarying warm weather. Gardeners in cooler climates such as Connecticut need to start them indoors in 3-inch pots about a month before the ground warms up. (See page 201.) In Zones 5 and 6, June is the recommended month for transplanting outdoors. I must confess, I seed melons *in place* in June and have had unusually good luck with them, but you can try out both methods.

Planting. Sweet melons require fertilizer-enriched soil to produce well. Here's the method I use: Dig out about 12 inches of soil. Fill the bottom 6 inches with an all-purpose fertilizer, such as 4-6-6 (follow application rates on label), plus a generous amount of compost or aged manure. Fill the hole with plain soil. Sow seeds 1 inch deep, or set transplants at the same level as they were growing in their pots.

If you plant in hills, sow four seeds to a hill, about 4 feet apart each way. Thin to two or three plants per hill when seedlings are about 4 inches high. If you prefer rows, space plants 18 inches apart and rows 6 feet apart. I don't plant in hills. I plant my melons in a single row, about 18 inches apart, and train them up a fence.

Growing needs. As the fruits grow heavy, I support them with individual slings. This keeps fruits off the ground and away from slugs and other pests that are attracted to the sweet fruit. The melons grow beautifully shaped and clean, and I can keep the soil well watered without spoiling the melons. It's a tremendous space-saver, too.

Melons need moist soil until the fruits begin to ripen. A thick mulch will reduce the amount of watering you need to do. In addition, I use the coffee can trick described on page 23, and my melons come out juicy and sweet. One year I didn't plant any melons and we bought them in the market; we were amazed at the difference in flavor and texture and decided to grow our own again the next season.

If you don't train vines up a fence, you'll find that empty coffee cans (or small plastic containers) come in handy as "fruit stands." Gently place each ripening fruit on its own upturned container to keep it dry and away from slugs. Some growers use plastic mulch with melons, but I don't want to have to get rid of the stuff at the end of the growing season.

Support melons by tying a panty-hose sling to a trellis or fence.

Pest potential. If striped cucumber beetles are pesky in your area, start your melons indoors to give the plants time to gain strength before they are attacked. With transplants it's much easier to keep ahead of the beetles by picking them off by hand whenever they appear. Young seedlings could be eaten up before you even realize the bugs are around. Row covers will protect plants from cucumber beetles, but you must remove them once flowers appear so bees can pollinate the flowers. For severe infestations, pyrethrins or rotenone provide control.

How to Harvest

Recognizing a ripe melon is a knack, and no one can really teach it to you. It takes experience. Aroma is one good test — a melon that smells fragrant and ready to eat usually is. With the cantaloupe types, the melon will slip easily from the vine when ready. Just give a little tug; if it's ready to be picked, it will come off in your hands. Maturity dates are only a limited guide. The moment of perfect ripeness is something you develop a sixth sense for, and some people are just better at it than others. Practice at your local farm stand, where you can ask advice and taste-test your choices.

Varieties

It's always nice to have a choice, and here you really do. Asian varieties of both cantaloupes and honeydews are available, with creamy white to golden rinds that are smooth or netted, and flesh ranging from pale green to salmon. They are all mouthwatering and freeze well for out-of-season enjoyment.

Varieties to look for: Hybrid Gold Sweet, Hybrid Jade King, Hybrid Golden Liner.

— CULINARY USES —

The options for using sweet melons in desserts, fruit salads, and so forth are too well known for me to detail here. Use these melons any way you would use honeydews and cantaloupes. Asian melons are even sweeter and more fragrant than the finest melons you have ever tasted.

Pickling Melon

Yue Gua, Uet Kwa

Cucumis melo Conomon Group

(color photo, page xi)

I n Asian countries, pickles are eaten not only because they're delicious, but because they're thought to be good for you. Most Americans aren't aware that there are such things as Asian pickles, yet the variety and number of them would turn Mr. Heinz green with envy. Almost every vegetable — cabbages, radishes, and turnips, as well as melons — finds its way into the Asian pickle barrel.

Here, to prove the point, is a melon grown just for pickling. Native to China and Japan, it's easy to grow in North America and lends itself to a wide variety of delicious pickles. If you like pickles, you'll love the Asian pickling melon.

Appearance

Pickling melons vary from dark to light green to silvery gray to white. They are oval in shape, about 12 inches long and 4 inches in diameter. The flesh is white and dense. Their close relationship to the common cucumber is evident both in their looks and in their flesh; cut in half they look almost exactly like a short, stubby cucumber with somewhat denser flesh and smaller seeds.

The plant spreads 10 or more feet, so you need a large garden to let pickling melon sprawl on the ground. A better method is to train it up a fence or trellis; this makes it easier to find the fruits, keeps them away from slugs, and reduces disease by allowing foliage and fruits to dry quickly. The foliage is dense enough to make a good windbreak; don't use it on all sides of an enclosed garden or you'll cut down on the air circulation within the garden.

How to Grow

Getting started. Pickling melons are a warm-weather crop. Sow the seeds in place when all danger of frost is past and the soil has warmed to at least 60°F. Pickling melons mature quickly (about 65 days), so you can grow them in just about any part of the United States. In Connecticut, June planting is usually reliable, except in an occasionally cool June. If an unexpected cool spell strikes, protect young seedlings with hot caps or row covers.

Pickling melon likes the same rich, fertile soil as cucumbers. Dig in plenty of compost and a balanced fertilizer before planting. (See my trick for boosting soil on page 30 under Planting.)

Planting. Sow seeds ½ inch deep, about 4 inches apart in rows; thin plants to 8 inches. Remember that plants can spread to 10 feet, so give the row plenty of room (or train plants up a trellis).

Growing needs. Side-dress when blossoms begin to turn to fruit, and every two weeks from then on. Alternatively, feed with fish-and-seaweed fertilizer. The vines are aggressive and need to be turned constantly in the direction you want them to grow. Let them go over the top of the fence and down the other side, if necessary; pinch off the tips when they get as long as you have room for. Water copiously; plants must never be allowed to dry out. A thick mulch will reduce the need to water.

How to Harvest

The time to harvest depends on the kind of pickle you want to make. Some Asian cooks prefer the young immature fruit; others say the melons must be mature. Even for mature fruit, don't allow melons to pass the point of just starting to whiten, as after this, they soon lose their good taste and get too dry. Pickling melons will ripen steadily over a period of four to six weeks, so you'll have ample time to try out a number of different ways of preparing this interesting vegetable.

Varieties

You won't find pickling melon in your average seed catalog; look for a company specializing in Asian vegetables.

Varieties to look for: Green Striped, Shimauri Stripe, Numame Early.

Pickling melons can be used in any standard pickle recipe. Don't limit yourself to sweet pickles; they make an unusual and delicious sour pickle. They take only a week in your refrigerator to reach the fully pickled stage. Or pickle like pearl onions in salt, vinegar, sugar, and chilis. These pickles take three months. If you can't wait that long, some Asian pickle recipes are ready to eat in just 24 hours.

Start with the shorter, simpler recipes, then work up to more elaborate ones. No pickle recipe is really complicated; some are a little lengthy, but most of that time is spent waiting for the pickles to mature. The hardest part of the pickle maker's job is having the patience to wait until the pickles are ready to eat.

MELON SOUPS. While this melon is grown primarily for pickling, it also can be cooked and eaten as a vegetable. Pickling melon has a particular affinity for seafood and makes a delicious fish soup. Simmer melon chunks in fish stock seasoned with soy sauce, sugar, and a little rice vinegar, until the melon is tender. Serve with a garnish of thinly sliced scallions as a starter to either an American or a Japanese meal. For a more filling soup, add chunks of cod.

Asian Cucumber

Qing Gua, Huang Gua, Tseng Kwa, Wong Gua

Cucumis sativus

(color photo, page x)

If you've ever grown cucumbers, you already know they are one of the easiest and most satisfying crops. I think cucumbers are great for children's gardens because they grow with such abandon and produce in such tremendous quantities. Where space is a problem, grow cucumbers up a fence or trellis; then the room they take up is air rather than ground space, and even a modest garden like mine can accommodate a number of different kinds. Now that I've discovered Asian cucumbers, I wonder why I took so long to try them.

Perhaps you've grown or eaten "burpless" cucumbers, a type with smaller-than-average seeds that is more digestible than the larger-seeded types. Sometimes these are described as less bitter. There's nothing new about the burpless cucumber; it's simply the type that's popular in Asia. It is sometimes also called Chinese cucumber or long cucumber.

Appearance

Asian cucumber plants look exactly like any other cucumbers. The vines, flowers, and leaves look so much alike that you need markers to tell them apart. The fruits, however, are noticeably different almost as soon as they begin to form. Characteristically, most Asian cucumbers are very slim. The long, slim cucumbers sold as burpless have the typical Asian cucumber shape.

The appearance of Asian cucumbers depends on how they're grown. Some grow curved on the ground but straight if grown on a support that allows them to hang free. Some will grow curved even on a fence, but the curve will be less pronounced. The serpent types may really startle you the first time you see one nestled under the leaves. They can grow curled around with the "head" raised inquiringly; others seem to be uncurling, ready to slither away. Even hanging free on the vine, they persist in curling into snakelike shapes. They are sweet, crisp, and delicious as well as fascinating to look at. Children love them.

How to Grow

Getting started. Like so many garden "rules," those for planting cucumbers can be stretched quite a bit. As long as you wait until the ground is completely warm, you can start them quite late and still get a good crop. I never have the patience to start cucumbers indoors. I sow them in the garden as soon after June 1 as I can manage, and my cucumbers seem to ripen just as fast as those of my friends who set out month-old seedlings at the same time.

Cucumbers want the same rich, fertile soil as their relatives, so dig in abundant compost and a balanced fertilizer before planting. (See page 23 for my method.) Test the soil pH and add lime as needed to correct acidity.

Planting. Sow seeds about 3 inches apart and ½ to ¾ inches deep. When the seedlings are 4 inches high, thin to about 12 inches apart; you can transplant if the best seedlings are not naturally spaced this way.

Growing needs. Cucumbers must be picked frequently. Grown on a trellis or a fence, a vine is much easier to scan for cucumbers and harvest. Vines grown on a fence also form an excellent windbreak.

DID YOU KNOW?

The origin of the cucumber is so ancient it's unknown; some think it first grew in India. It was introduced to China well before written history and was found in Egyptian tombs dating from the Twelfth Dynasty. The Romans were inordinately fond of it. Charlemagne gave it a favored place in his fabulous garden, and it is one of the vegetables mentioned in the Bible.

If your cucumbers are bitter, you've let them get too dry; it's as simple as that. Always water copiously. Cucumbers sometimes worry new gardeners when the leaves wilt dramatically in hot weather, but well-watered plants recover fully by the next morning. Water regularly in hot weather — every three days is not too often if rain is scarce. The moisture content of the soil deep down around the roots is more important than the surface moisture content. Once plants reach a foot tall, a thick mulch helps to conserve soil moisture.

If your cucumbers are bitter after a dry spell, pick off all the ones maturing at that time, then water well and regularly. Your new batch of cucumbers will be sweet and back to normal.

A midsummer side-dressing of compost and fertilizer will keep your vines producing generously.

Pest and disease potential. If you have trouble with insects, hand-picking is the best recourse. You can keep insects away early in the season with row covers, but remove them as soon as plants begin to flower. I've never had a problem with diseases on cucumbers, perhaps because I grow them on a support. The best way to deal with diseases is to grow resistant varieties, but don't worry about this unless you or your neighbors have had a problem.

How to Harvest

You can pick cucumbers at any stage in their growth before maturity. You *must* pick the cucumbers before they mature or the vines will relax, work done, and stop producing. If you miss a cucumber and it turns yellow, that vine may stop forming new cukes.

It's not easy to spot all the cucumbers. Daily harvesting is your best bet, especially as Asian cucumbers are so slim they're easy to overlook. Any small cucumber can be pickled, so pick them young if the harvest is beginning to swamp you with more cucumbers than you can manage.

Varieties

Unlike some Chinese vegetables, cucumbers offer a wide choice and are carried by many suppliers. Not all catalogs identify them as Asian, but any burpless cucumber is basically Asian, and any long, slim type probably is, too. Cucumbers called "Armenian," "Syrian," or "Turkish" share the characteristics of Asian cucumbers.

To learn about the different varieties quickly, grow several next season. I grew five different kinds one year and had a wonderful time. Some are early, some a little later, but all are prolific and delicious. Have fun!

Varieties to look for: Hybrid Crisp Winner, Hybrid Malai, Hybrid White Star.

Surprisingly enough, most people don't appreciate how to use cucumbers. I can see your eyebrows going up, but most cucumbers in the United States are eaten raw in salads, or possibly served with sour cream (as in Russia) or in yogurt (as in the Middle East), but even that barely scratches the surface.

SLICED AND MARINATED. In both Japan and Germany, cucumbers are served thinly sliced and marinated in a slightly sweetened vinegar, then drained and set out as a relish at almost any main meal. For an easy marinade, use 1 cup water, ½ cup vinegar, 2 teaspoons sugar, and a pinch of salt; let sit for about an hour. In Japan, the vinegar will be rice vinegar and the salt may be in the form of soy sauce, but the basic recipe is similar. I prefer cider vinegar for its snap; you may prefer white vinegar. This is a refreshing and easy pickle, good for unexpected guests because it is so quick.

STUFFED. Stuffed cucumbers make a good summer salad, a great dish for a buffet. To stuff:

1. Take a slice off each end, and scoop out the seeds with a small spoon.

2. Fill the cavity with any of the following: anchovies, celery, and hard-boiled eggs in curried mayonnaise; shrimp, bean sprouts, and chives in dill yogurt; red caviar, minced onion, and sour cream (these are just a few suggestions).

3. Wrap the cucumbers in plastic and chill thoroughly in the refrigerator.

4. To serve, slice ½-inch thick and arrange on leaf lettuce or thin slices of French bread; melba rounds will work, too.

SAUTÉED. Cooking cucumbers offers the most surprises. Peeled, seeded, diced, and sautéed for 3 minutes in sesame oil, sprinkled with chopped chives, and simmered in ½ cup chicken broth, cucumbers turn translucent, like pickled watermelon rind. The beautiful pale green contrasts with the dark green of the chives to make an Asian picture. Cucumbers cooked in this fashion stay crisp and are very digestible; even people who think they can't eat or don't like cucumbers will enjoy them this way. (In fact, many of your guests won't even recognize what vegetable they're eating.)

COOKED WITH YOGURT, MEATS, AND OTHER VEGETABLES. For another quick company dish try this:

1. Combine shredded cooked pork with sliced cucumbers (peeled and seeded), thinly sliced scallions, and julienned strips of boiled ham.

2. Sauté the vegetables for 3 minutes in oil. Add a bit of freshly grated ginger, a little turmeric, and a hint of ground cloves. Add all other ingredients, and heat briefly.

3. Turn heat down low, and stir in a cup of yogurt. Reheat (but do not boil) and serve immediately.

This should be a very meaty dish and is good with rice and greens. It's a great recipe for leftovers. Use chicken, fish, or beef instead of the pork, and other vegetables can be used.

Chinese Pumpkin

Nan Gua, Nam Gua

Cucurbita maxima, C. moschata

(color photo, page x)

The only problem you'll encounter in growing Chinese pumpkins is what to call them. "Pumpkin" and "squash" are used interchangeably to describe these vegetables. In the United States, "pumpkin" is almost never used to describe winter squashes, but "squash" is sometimes used to describe pumpkins. You may also find these vegetables called Oriental pumpkin, Oriental squash, Asian squash, or kabocha.

Appearance

Chinese pumpkins don't look like the pumpkins common in North America; they come in all shapes and various colors. The rind may be dark green, orange, brown, or almost gray, with or without stripes, and often deeply ridged. The flesh varies in color from orange to yellow and is usually very sweet. Some varieties are quite warty; all are very decorative and attractive enough to include in autumnal table decorations. Most have rather large sprawling vines and require more space than summer squash. They will climb on anything and can be sown among corn or up a fence or trellis.

How to Grow

Getting started. In cool climates, start seeds indoors about 4 weeks before the ground warms up. Or, if you have a long enough growing season, just sow them in place once all danger of frost has passed and the soil has warmed to 55°F or 60°F.

Planting. Winter squash are traditionally planted in rows or hills, but planting them along a fence or other support is a space-saver for small gardens. If planted in this fashion, the seeds should be sown 1 inch deep, three to four to every foot. Thin them to 18 to 36 inches apart as soon as seedlings are about 3 inches long.

Growing needs. Incorporate lots of compost and some all-purpose fertilizer before sowing the seeds. A balanced organic fertilizer or traditional formula such as 4-6-6 mixed with compost will give good results. (Follow the recommended amounts on the fertilizer package.) Don't feed too much nitrogen from then on or you'll create vines that are overlong and easily broken. Regular *light* feeding with a diluted fertilizer, such as liquid seaweed, is advisable.

Like all cucurbits, Chinese pumpkins require constant moisture. As the vines grow, they shade the earth beneath them and make it easier to keep it moist. If you don't use a thick mulch, you may have to water every day in dry weather.

Pest potential. Dusting the leaves and soil around plants with wood ashes may help discourage insect pests. Control cucumber beetles (see advice on page 31), as these can carry bacterial wilt.

How to Harvest

For longer storage, harvest winter squash before the first frost. Wait until vines have begun to die back, so the skins will have hardened somewhat. Cut squash from vines with an inch or two of stem attached. Dry in the sun for a few days (until the stems shrivel) to toughen skins.

DID YOU KNOW?

The Asian types of what we call winter squash are highly esteemed in China. There the pumpkin is known as the "emperor of the garden" and is a symbol of fertility (which anyone who has ever grown this prolific vine can easily understand) and good health. Pumpkin and squash seeds are high in protein and a rich source of iron, zinc, and phosphorus.

Varieties

Many catalogs carry at least one form of Chinese pumpkins, but you may not find it labeled as such. Look for these under winter squashes. 'Hokkaido' is a reliable round, slate green variety, with fruits that weigh about 5 pounds. 'Red Kuri', also known as 'Orange Hokkaido', is closely related to the big blue-gray 'Hubbard' squash. Regardless of the variety, they all take about 100 days to mature.

Other varieties to look for: Asian Gold, Hybrid Papaya Golden, Hybrid Sunday Sweet.

STORING CHINESE PUMPKINS

Chinese pumpkins store very well and, under the right conditions, will last through the winter. Cure them in the sun for several days (cover them at night or take them in out of the dew) to toughen their skins. Store them in a cool, dry place; a temperature of 45°F to 50°F will hold them well. Check them over every so often. They will keep for months as long as the skin is not bruised or punctured.

Chinese pumpkins can be used in all the ways you use other winter squash or pumpkins — in soups and pies, puréed, baked, or fried.

SOUP. Chinese pumpkin makes an unusual soup, beautiful in color with a delicate flavor. Peel, seed, slice, and boil in a little salted water until tender. Drain and purée in a blendor. Meanwhile, brown a chopped onion; add this to the squash with pepper, salt, and a little curry powder. Stir in a cup of yogurt, and reheat without boiling. Garnish with thinly sliced raw water chestnuts when serving.

PURÉED. Mixed with eggs, puréed Chinese pumpkin makes a vegetable custard — just follow a standard recipe for corn pudding. This is not a dessert, but it could be if you add sugar and nutmeg with a pinch of cloves. Put it in a pie shell, and garnish with whipped cream laced with sherry. Chinese pumpkin has a richer flavor than our common pumpkin, so it makes a tastier pie when used in traditional pumpkin pie recipes.

JAPANESE-STYLE SOUP. For a very easy Japanese dish, cut peeled pumpkin into chunks. Add the chunks to chicken broth, as well as a little dashi (available from Asian markets), and simmer for 30 minutes. Then add sugar, soy sauce, and salt to taste. Simmer until the pumpkin is tender. During the last 3 minutes of cooking, add Japanese noodles.

IRISH-STYLE STEW. Irish lamb stew with potatoes, onions, carrots, and chunks of winter squash is another tasty but easy dish to prepare.

STIR-FRY. To stir-fry winter squash, peel, seed, and cut it into small chunks. Blanch in water for 10 minutes, drain, and cook in peanut oil with bamboo shoots, scallions, and snow peas; at the last minute add mizuna. Stir in soy sauce just before serving. This is especially good with toasted sesame seeds sprinkled over each portion.

Luffa

LING JIAO SI GUA, YOU LIN SI GUA
Luffa acutangula

TSEE GWA, SI GUA
L. cylindrical

(color photo, page x)

No single vegetable I can think of produces as much useful material as the luffa, also known as loofah. "Material" sounds like an odd way to describe a vegetable, but luffa is much more than a vegetable. All parts of the plant except the root are good for either culinary or household use.

Luffa grows rampantly with little care; a single vine will produce over 25 large gourds. You may already know luffa as an ornamental gourd without realizing that it's also a fine vegetable. If so, you're in for a pleasant surprise when you taste it. Both of these species are also known by several other common names: *L. acutangula* is sometimes called ridged skin luffa, angled luffa, or Chinese okra; you may find *L. cylindrical* called sponge luffa, smooth luffa, dishrag gourd, or vegetable sponge. The gourds are much larger than okra but have the same sort of pronounced ridges.

Luffa was brought to China long before records were kept. Today it's grown throughout the world, especially in tropical and semitropical countries.

Appearance

Like many cucurbits, luffa is a vine. It grows rampantly and is best trained on a trellis, where it will take up much less space than sprawling on the ground. Some varieties can reach 15 feet in length, with numerous pretty, bright yellow flowers. The gourds are deeply ridged, like oversized okra, sometimes slightly curved and sometimes straight. You'll get straighter gourds if you grow the vine on a trellis or fence so they hang free. The gourds vary in length; longer varieties can grow over 24 inches long and weigh up to 5 pounds; smaller varieties usually grow to about 12 inches.

How to Grow

Getting started. Luffa is a warm-weather plant and can't be set out until the soil is thoroughly warm. Allow about 115 days to maturity. If you can't be sure of uniformly warm weather for that long in your area, start the seeds indoors a month in advance. Luffa is not as delicate as it sounds. It grows successfully in Maine, so give it a try.

Luffa is a heavy feeder and benefits from a generous application of compost and all-purpose fertilizer before planting. (See my recommendation for enriching the soil on page 23.) The pH should be slightly alkaline, so a little

PREPARING LUFFA SPONGES

Once you've harvested all the young fruit you want to eat, let the remaining gourds mature, then remove and put in hot water. You don't have to keep the water hot, but change it daily. When the outside skin begins to rot away, remove it and you'll see the inside is a spongy fibrous mass. Dry the individual gourds in the sun and eureka! You have a vegetable "sponge." This is the famous loofah of Egypt. It's great as a back-scrubber in the shower and gives the skin a gentle glow without ever being abrasive. I've always kept one in the shower, but it was years before I knew what it was or that I could grow it

Many of luffa's common names tell you some of its household uses. Because it's a good scrubber, both cooks and gardeners find endless uses for it. It doesn't get offensive or retain odors, like synthetic sponges, and it's good for cleaning dishes, pots and pans, flower pots, and plastic seed trays. It won't scratch no matter how hard you press. It has innumerable other uses, too. In Asia, it has been used to make bedroom slippers, floor and table mats, and as stuffing for pillows and mattresses.

lime or wood ashes may be in order if soil tests show your soil is acidic.

Planting. Outdoors, plant seeds 1 inch deep; sow two to three seeds every 2 to 3 feet, and thin to one plant in each spot. There just doesn't seem to be any advantage to hills. Unless you have an enormous garden, I suggest you grow luffa along a fence or trellis. In this case, sow seeds about 3 to 6 inches apart and thin to 24 inches apart. Tie the vines to their support as soon as they can reach it. (I prefer to plant everything possible in rows along a fence, even spaghetti squash, cucumbers, and watermelons.)

Growing needs. It may take two weeks for the seeds to germinate; keep the soil moist during that time. If nights turn cool, protect with row covers. Once the seedlings are up, side-dress every three weeks with an all-purpose fertilizer, or feed with fish-and-seaweed fertilizer.

Remove all of the first flowers when they are still in bud; these make good eating. If any gourds develop but don't look healthy, remove those also. By doing this, you increase fruit production and ensure a uniformly usable crop.

This is a thirsty as well as a hungry plant, so keep it well watered. In most areas, rainfall will not be sufficient. A thick mulch reduces the need to water.

How to Harvest

There are two harvest periods — early for the immature vegetable, late for the mature "sponge." For eating, pick the gourds when they are 4 to 6 inches long. Since you can figure on about 25 gourds per vine, you won't need many mature vines. If you need garden space for fall crops, pull up some vines once the vegetable harvest is completed.

Varieties

Since it's commonly grown in this country as an ornamental gourd, you may find luffa listed under "flowers" in seed catalogs or under "edible gourds." Most suppliers carry one of two species: *Luffa cylindrical* or *L. acutangula*. Several varieties of each species are available. Both are edible and grown as food throughout the world; both form good sponges. Of the two, *L. cylindrical* is thought to be tastier. Since it's much larger, it's also more useful in the household.

Luffas are sometimes referred to as ridge gourds. The smaller species, *L. acutangula,* is known as angled luffa and early ridge gourd.

Varieties to look for: Luffa acutangula: Summer Long, Hybrid Green Glory, Lucky Boy; *L. cylindrical:* Hybrid Summer Cross, Hybrid Smooth Beauty, Southern Winner.

LEAVES AND FLOWERS. Both the leaves and flower buds of luffa are edible when very young. Simmer in boiling salted water until just tender, then toss with butter that has been heated with a pinch of curry powder.

FRUITS. The fruit is edible only when immature. It can be prepared exactly like zucchini (although it doesn't taste like zucchini), which gives you a wide range of recipes to choose from. It is delicious sliced or diced and tossed in a salad, like cucumber. The flavor is delicately sweet, and everyone seems to like it. Always cut off the ridges with a paring knife to prepare the gourds for eating; the skin can be left on. You can also:

- Try it stuffed with a mix of browned chopped meat and vegetables, and baked in a 350°F oven for an hour.

- Simmer until tender and serve with butter and a teaspoon of lemon juice; it will taste something like early English peas.

- Stir-fry it, Chinese-style, in sesame oil with bamboo shoots, snow peas, scallions, water chestnuts, soy sauce, and grated fresh ginger. For a heartier dish, add shredded chicken, pork, or beef. Or dice and stir-fry with shrimp, scallions, and a finely chopped green chili.

- Simmer briefly in a clear soup, or deep-fry as tempura.

SEEDS. Try oven-roasting the seeds of the mature gourd (lightly salted and oiled, if you like) for a nutritious snack.

DRIED GOURD. The Chinese consider the dried gourd a special culinary treat. To make this, slice the young gourds and sun- or oven-dry. Store in tightly covered jars (checking occasionally to make sure there is no mold). These are especially prized when cooked in broth, but they can be combined with other vegetables and meats as you would ordinarily use squash.

Bitter Melon

Ku Gua, Foo Gwa
Momordica charantia
(color photo, page x)

This is not, as you might suppose, something you eat as a fruit. Botanically speaking, it's a fruit because it contains seeds, but your taste buds will consider it a vegetable. It's more closely related to gourds than to our familiar cantaloupes, honeydews, and other melons.

Barely known in the United States, bitter melon is grown in both North and South America as an ornamental vine. Its edible qualities may come as a surprise to many a gardener who has looked at but not eaten its attractive foliage and strange fruits. It is also known as bitter gourd, balsam pear, and kerala.

Appearance

Since bitter melon is often grown as an ornamental, you know it must be good-looking. It's a handsome vine with attractively lobed, bright green leaves and numerous small, cheerful yellow flowers. The melons are really odd-looking. They grow up to 12 inches long, about 2 inches in diameter, and are oval but taper to a point at each end. When immature, the fruits are yellowish green or dark green. As they mature, they turn the same bright yellow as the flowers, then bright orange. Plants are very showy when fully fruited. If allowed to ripen, the melon will split open; the inside it reveals is even more striking than the flowers and fruits. This is a fascinating plant to grow and to eat.

How to Grow

Getting started. Bitter melon, like most melons, is a warm-weather crop. Wait to sow seeds outdoors until all danger of frost is past and the ground is thoroughly warm. Or you can start them indoors two weeks before the last frost and grow them indoors for a month before setting out. (See page 201.)

Planting. Bitter melon grows best with some sort of support. Sow seeds next to a fence or trellis 1 inch deep, 6 to 8 inches apart. A well-fertilized soil, high in nitrogen, will suit it best. The seeds are slow to germinate (up to 14 days), so be patient. Keep the seedbed moist until seedlings appear.

Growing needs. Copious watering is required throughout the growing season. To make this easier, dig a ditch next to the planted row to catch more water. Water every four days if the season is dry; deep watering is the only kind that will do any good.

Bitter melon is a heavy feeder; it requires a good deal of fertilizer. Side-dress plants every couple of weeks, or water with half-strength fish-and-seaweed fertilizer. Dusting the vines with wood ashes or using a wood-ash mulch may help deter pests. (Don't try this if your soil is alkaline, though.)

When vines are about 10 inches long, tie them to their support. From then on, you can weave new growth in and out

Tie the vine to the trellis and weave new growth in and out. To provide the extra water that bitter melons need, dig a ditch next to the planted row to catch water.

of the support. For the most ornamental effect, tie it in such a way as to train the foliage where you want it to go.

How to Harvest

While you're waiting for the melons to ripen, you can harvest the young leaves and cook them as greens. For the best eating and the least bitterness, fruits should be picked when immature, no more than 6 inches long. If you find you like the taste very much, you can try letting the melons mature a bit longer, until you reach your limit of bitterness.

The younger the melon, the longer it must be cooked to get tender; older melons cook up more quickly. Once the fruits lose their green color, you won't want to eat them. You can let the melons mature completely, both for the ornamental effect and for next year's seed crop.

Varieties

Varieties to look for: Taiwan Large, Hong Kong Green, Hybrid White Pearl.

DID YOU KNOW?

Bitter melon is one of those vegetables for which there's no equivalent in the roster of our Western foods. As you may gather from its name, its flavor is definitely bitter; at first it startles the taste buds, then it becomes a delight. The bitterness is due to the presence of quinine. (Because of this ingredient, the dried melon has been used in Chinese medicines.) If you like tonic water or the Bitter Lemon soft drink from England (both contain quinine), you will surely like this vegetable. Even if you don't, make room for it in your kitchen, as you'll find its flavor a welcome change.

CLASSIC CHINESE BEAN DISH. A classic Chinese dish is bitter melon prepared with fermented black beans. Any market that carries Chinese foods will have these prepared soybeans; they are called *dow sei*. Here's how to make the dish:

1. Soak the fermented beans in water for 10 minutes before using, as they are heavily salted.

2. To make the sauce, combine the fermented black beans with minced garlic and set aside.

3. Cut the unpeeled melon in half and remove the seeds to make room for stuffing.

4. To make the stuffing, combine raw minced pork, raw minced shrimp, finely chopped water chestnuts, soy sauce, cornstarch, and sugar; blend with the bean and garlic mixture. Fill the cavity with these combined ingredients. Heap the stuffing high because it will shrink in cooking.

5. Cook until the melon is tender. Steaming the stuffed halves will take about 40 minutes.

Alternative. Slice the unpeeled melon, remove the seeds, dip the slices in cornstarch, lightly brown on both sides in a little sesame oil, then steam until tender. You can also bake or braise the cut melon halves.

If you haven't used up all the black beans, stir-fry them with minced garlic in sesame oil for 1 minute and store them in the refrigerator. They are called for in many other Chinese dishes.

STIR–FRY. A quick and easy-to-prepare Chinese dish is stir-fried melon and chicken. If very bitter, first parboil the melon for 3 minutes. Then cut both chicken and melon into small chunks. Stir-fry melon for 1 minute, add chicken, and fry a few minutes more. Add soy sauce, minced garlic, ginger, and a bit of chicken broth, and reheat, stirring to blend. If you prefer less garlic flavor, add the garlic when you first cook the melon.

(continued on next page)

COOKED GREENS (LEAVES). The young leaves of bitter melon can be steamed and used as cooked greens. Do not eat the seeds. They are a strong purgative (an especially strong type of laxative) and definitely not something to sample.

RELISH. Parboiled bitter melon can be made into a tangy relish that's especially good served with a flaky white-fleshed fish. Marinate the parboiled melon for 2 hours in rice or cider vinegar mixed with an equal amount of water, a little sugar, and a pinch of salt. Drain the melon, slice thinly, and serve.

OTHER USES. For an American dish, try parboiling bitter melon for 5 minutes, then adding it to a skillet of braised veal and carrots for the last 30 minutes of cooking. For a quick Chinese soup, simmer small chunks of bitter melon in chicken broth until tender.

3

THE CHINESE BEANS

SOYBEAN • FAVA BEAN • ADZUKI BEAN • MUNG
BEAN • YARD-LONG BEAN

In parts of the world where the standard of living is not as high and consumption of meat not as great as in the United States, beans are the staff of life. Whenever a new bean is rediscovered, it quickly spreads around the world and takes hold in whatever countries and climates can grow it. Beans take up little room and are high in protein, vitamins, minerals, and overall food value. Beans keep well; they're easy to dry or freeze. Versatile, they combine well with herbs and spices to suit many cuisines. The cost of food may once again cause Americans to lower their meat consumption and beans to come into their own. What better time to discover the delicious Chinese beans? They're as easy to grow as the ubiquitous green bean, and all of these beans are readily available from seed catalogs.

Soybean

Mao Dou, Wong Dau

Glycine max

(color photo, page xi)

If you've looked for a cholesterol-free alternative to steak, had an allergy to cheese, always longed for your own milk cow, or got bored with all the green vegetables you know but can't think of a new one, the soybean is the answer. It can lower your budget, improve your health, and provide welcome variety to your diet.

You'll shine as a gardener, be acclaimed as a versatile cook, and join the millions of people around the world who depend on soybeans for much of the quality and nutrition of their food. Soybeans are excellent sources of protein and supply omega-3 fatty acids as well. They are sometimes called *da tou*.

Soybeans are probably used in more ways than any other vegetable. They're eaten both as a green vegetable (known by its Japanese name, *edamame*) and as a dried bean. They are the source of soy milk, a good substitute for cow's milk, as you already know if you're allergic to cow's milk. (The soybean has been called the "cow of the East.") You can buy cheeses made from soy milk. More common is the bean curd known as tofu. Soy sauce is made from fermented soybeans; miso, the Japanese paste used for seasoning, is also made from fermented soybeans.

Soybeans can be ground into soy flour (good for boosting the protein content of baked goods) or pressed to make soy oil. This is one of the most common vegetable oils among the dozens of ingredients listed on processed-food products. The roasted beans are also used to make a caffeine-free beverage that smells like coffee, even if the taste is hardly pure Colombian. As if all that weren't enough, manufacturers use soybeans in the making of "thick shakes" and other "nondairy" foods, linoleum, shampoo, paint, and many other items of our everyday life.

Appearance

Soybeans come in a fairly wide range of colors: black, green, gray, yellow, brown, and white, some with eyes of a contrasting color, some solid. Regardless of the color of the mature bean, the plants all look very similar, though there are some variations in the size of the bush. Maturity dates, on the other hand, vary considerably.

The beans are about the size of limas, though not as flat, and grow three or four to a pod. One seed catalog gave an estimate that one plant of a particular variety produces about 50 beans, so that's a useful general guideline.

How to Grow

Getting started. Soybeans are a warm-weather crop, so wait to plant until the soil has completely warmed up. Early planting is useless as the seeds will rot in the ground. If the variety you want to grow requires a longer growing season than your area, start them indoors. (See page 201.) Figure back from your earliest fall frost date to determine when to start the seedlings; transplant into the garden when the ground is warm and all danger of frost is past.

Soybeans grow best in fertile soil that is neutral to slightly acidic. Add limestone if necessary to bring soil pH to about 6.5 (no higher). If liming is necessary, it should be done at least two weeks before seeds are planted. Incorporate compost and a balanced fertilizer about a week before seeding.

Planting. Sow seeds 1½ to 2 inches deep, 2 to 5 inches apart in rows and 24 to 30 inches apart.

Growing needs. Soybeans are trouble-free and need almost no attention except for regular watering. Keep the soil on the moist side throughout the growing season. If you mixed fertilizer into the soil before planting, no more should be necessary.

If plants get very tall you may need to stake them, because they bear profusely and the weight of the pods may pull them over. You don't need to stake when planting out (as with tomatoes); since you won't need heavy stakes, putting them in later won't cause much disturbance to the roots.

How to Harvest

Harvest twice: once for green shelling, once for dried beans.

For edamame. For the green-shelling stage, pick when the beans are fully grown within the pods but before they turn yellow. Generally this is about 30 days before the maturity date, but weather conditions can speed or delay this stage, so keep an eye on your crop.

For dried beans. The dried stage is easy to recognize: The plants and pods turn completely brown. They look dead and ready for the compost heap. Pull up the plants by their roots and let them finish drying under cover.

Varieties

You'll find that some varieties are particularly recommended for green-shelling (edamame), others for drying, and some for sprouting. Grow some of each and see if you agree with the recommendations. Any kind can serve all uses regardless of what it is specially recommended for.

Varieties to look for: Taiwame, Green Legend, Late Giant Black Seeded.

DID YOU KNOW?

Soybean roots harbor nitrogen-fixing bacteria, so the dry bushes are a valuable source of this essential plant nutrient and provide it in a highly usable form. While you can compost plants after removing the beans, you'll retain more of the nitrogen if you dig or till the spent soybean plants directly into your garden soil. Stash the foliage in a corner of your garden if you can't dig it under right away. If you ever take a year off from your garden or want the soil to lie fallow, plant soybeans and simply rototill them under at the end of the season.

SOYBEAN SPROUTS. In your kitchen, you may already have used soybeans to make your own bean sprouts. They're worth growing if only for this purpose, providing a fresh vegetable even in midwinter.

GREEN SOYBEANS, IN PODS. Cook the green soybeans (edamame) in their pods until tender. Drain, season with salt or soy sauce, and serve while still warm. In Japan, diners each squeeze their own pods, popping the beans directly into their mouths. You don't need to add any butter or oil because the beans have such a high oil content.

GREEN SOYBEANS, SHELLED. You'll find the flavor of soybeans mild but nutty and very agreeable. To shell them, blanch pods briefly in boiling salted water, for about 5 minutes; let cool enough to handle and shell. Once shelled you can:

- Reheat the beans in a little broth, soy sauce, and sherry until tender, about 15 minutes.

- Cook like baby limas and combine with corn for an Asian succotash.

- Cream them, if you like creamed beans, and add a little grated ginger to the cream sauce.

- Try them roasted and lightly salted, like peanuts.

JAPANESE-STYLE SOYBEANS. A popular Japanese festival dish is made with cooked soybeans.

1. Simmer the cooked beans for 10 minutes in equal parts sugar and water, plus a pinch of salt.

2. Remove from the heat and let stand overnight at room temperature.

3. In the morning, stir in a spoonful of soy sauce and reheat until the bean mixture thickens and all the moisture is absorbed.

4. Serve at room temperature with broiled chicken breasts, a flaky fish, or — with the addition of grated radish — as a dip for tempura vegetables. You can also use it as a dessert or as a filling for pastries.

Fava Bean

CAN DOU, TSAAM DOU
Vicia faba
(color photo, page xi)

The fava is only distantly related to limas, green beans, kidneys, and other beans. Its closest relative is vetch, and its Latin genus name shows this: Vicia rather than Phaseolus or Vigna. But for all practical culinary purposes, fava is a true bean. It looks like a bean, grows like a bean, dries like a bean, and for thousands of years it was the only bean known to European kitchens. It is also called broad bean.

Appearance

Fava beans are bush beans, but the bush is quite tall compared to other bush-type beans. Under ideal conditions, they grow 4 feet tall. The pods are borne in profusion and are larger than green beans, 7 to 12 inches long. The beans are light green, large, and very flat, something like limas but more angular. There are rarely more than five to seven beans in a pod. The flowers, as with most beans, are not very conspicuous and are the usual white.

How to Grow

Getting started. Growing fava beans gives you a chance to get a jump on your bean crop because they are much hardier than green beans. In spring, you can plant them as soon as the ground can be worked. Unlike other beans, favas do not thrive in hot weather (one of the reasons they're so successful in England). In the United States, we can approximate the English climate by planting in very early spring in cool-climate areas and in the fall for a spring crop in warmer regions. Their upright habit and early short season make fava beans particularly suited to succession cropping. Plant favas when you plant your snow peas and you'll be able to replace them with green beans, cabbages, beets, and similar vegetables.

Planting. Fava beans grow best in a rich soil with plenty of moisture. Dig in compost and some balanced fertilizer before planting. The large seeds are easy to handle. Sow them 1 to 1½ inches deep, 4 to 6 inches apart, and in rows 18 to 36 inches apart.

Growing needs. When the pods begin to form, side-dress with the same mixture you used when sowing. Keep well watered and you'll have no problems (unless you have an early, hot summer).

DID YOU KNOW?

Fava beans have been found with Bronze Age artifacts in Switzerland and Italy; they are depicted on Egyptian tombs and mentioned in the *Iliad*; archeologists unearthed them on the site of ancient Troy. The Romans offered fava beans, along with bread and circuses, to the populace, who then used them as ballots for voting. By the first century A.D., fava beans had been introduced to China, whose people have regarded them highly ever since.

For most people, fava beans are an excellent addition to the diet; they are very high in protein and folate, and lower in calories than other beans. They are also a good source of iron, phosphorus, and other minerals.

Some people of Mediterranean ancestry carry a genetic allergy to raw and under-cooked beans. If you're one of these unlucky people, you won't be able to eat them unless you're careful to cook them thoroughly. Fava beans are nonetheless very popular in Italy, Portugal, and Spain.

How to Harvest

You can harvest fava beans at three different stages: as edible pods, edible shell beans, and dried beans.

For edible pods. Begin picking as soon as the pods have started to show the bare outline of the beans. At this point, you can eat the entire pod, as described on facing page.

For shelled beans. Let beans plump up before harvesting as fresh shell beans.

For dried beans. Let pods mature and dry before harvesting the fully mature beans for drying. Beans reach the mature stage anywhere from 65 to 90 days, depending on the variety.

I think it's a waste to freeze fava beans; I prefer to save my freezer space for other vegetables. Eat them fresh while they're available and then contain yourself until the next crop. Meanwhile enjoy all the wonderful things you can do with dried fava beans.

Varieties

Because of their immense popularity, fava beans are carried by many seed catalogs.

Varieties to look for: Aquadulce, Broad Windsor, Precoce Violetto.

COOKED YOUNG PODS. The very young pods of fava beans are deliciously edible, a treat available only to the gardener who grows them. In no time at all, however, the pods pass the point of edibility and become useful only as a container for the beans. If you pride yourself on being a gourmet, don't pass up the chance to enjoy these beans in this special way. Just cook the fava pods as you would snow peas: stir-fry or simmer briefly in boiling salted water.

YOUNG BEANS, SHELLED AND COOKED. To enjoy fava beans at the next-to-earliest, just past the edible-pod stage, shell them like peas and cook them just as tenderly. Some say they even taste like peas, but I'm reluctant to ascribe the taste of a familiar vegetable to an unfamiliar one. They taste like their delicious selves.

OLDER BEANS, SHELLED AND COOKED. If you've waited a little longer to pick and shell them, remove the outer parchmentlike skin on the individual bean. This is easiest if you blanch the beans, then rub with a dish towel or peel with a sharp knife. Once peeled, cook just like the immature beans, until tender. Then you can:

- Drain them well and serve with heavy cream and a little summer savory.

- Make an excellent purée by cooking them with salt, black pepper, and thinly sliced scallions. Or make a deliciously thick fava bean soup, redolent of thyme and basil, as a warm welcome to guests on a winter's day.

DRIED BEANS. Since they have a short season in Connecticut, I am particularly grateful that fava beans dry beautifully, just as other beans do, and can be kept indefinitely in this state. With dried beans you can:

- Cook them like navy beans in casseroles and other slow-cooking dishes.

- Simmer until tender and add to rice-and-vegetable medleys along with a bit of basil, a few tomatoes, tomato paste, and some chopped onion.

Adzuki Bean

Xiao Hong Dou, Siu Huhng Dau

Vigna angularis

(color photo, page xi)

Adzuki beans have been cultivated in Asia for thousands of years. Also known as aduki beans or red beans, the Japanese call them azuki. They have a somewhat sweeter flavor than most beans, and this has led to their use in Asian desserts.

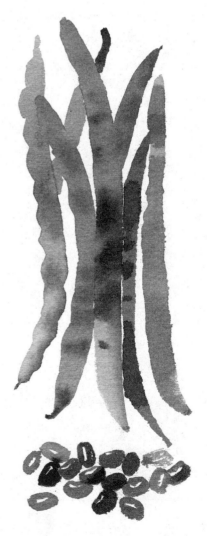

The adzuki bean is almost as complete a food as the soybean and, to my way of thinking, much better tasting. Adzuki beans are very high in protein. They are also rich in minerals and almost all of the amino acids, including lysine. They cook faster and may be easier to digest than other beans.

Appearance

The plant forms a 2-foot-high bush, something like green beans. The young pods — shorter than green beans — are borne in profusion. When the pods are mature, shelling them reveals the shiny, red, round beans. If you prefer, you can dry the beans in the pods, without shelling, and then shell as wanted. This takes up more storage space, so I find it impractical.

How to Grow

Getting started. Plant the same time as green beans, about two weeks after the last frost date when the ground has warmed up. You can plant successive crops, just as with green beans, by sowing a new row each week. Adzukis grow best with cool nights, but they're fairly resilient. They thrive in slightly acidic soil (as do most vegetables except peas and beets). It's not worth worrying a lot about this unless you're going for the highest possible yield.

Planting. Sow seeds ½ to 1 inch deep in rich, loamy soil. Sow 2 to 3 inches apart in rows 18 to 30 inches apart; there is no need to thin.

Growing needs. Keep the watering consistent and ample. Fertilize after seedlings are about 4 to 5 inches high and again when flowers start to form pods.

How to Harvest

For green beans. To harvest as green beans, pick when the beans are just beginning to show in the pod. Pick every five or six days or they'll get away from you. If you do miss some and they start to ripen, let them do so, and sow another row for fresh eating.

For dried beans. Allow adzuki beans to mature fully (about 120 days: check your seed catalog or packet for specific advice) to harvest for dried beans. Wait to harvest until pods turn dry and brown and the seeds rattle inside. Once dried, keep beans in a tightly covered jar and they'll last indefinitely.

Varieties

Only one variety is widely available. You may find adzukis listed under "sprouting beans" in seed catalogs. Once you have grown them successfully you may want to save some of your own seeds for next year's crop.

DID YOU KNOW?

Adzuki beans make particularly delectable bean sprouts; they have a nutty flavor quite different from mung beans. (See page 68 for sprouting directions.)

FRESH BEANS. Adzuki beans make an excellent fresh vegetable. Pick young, like snow peas, and eat them pod and all. Just cook briefly in a little boiling water or sauté for 3 minutes in sesame oil. A dash of soy sauce and maybe a pinch of freshly grated ginger, and you have an unusual company dish that everyone will like. Or cook any way you cook common green beans.

PURÉED. A handy ingredient to have in your refrigerator is puréed adzuki beans. Simmer dried beans in boiling salted water until tender, drain well, and purée in the blender. Mix with minced garlic, a pinch of turmeric or Chinese mustard, and a bit of grated ginger, and serve hot as a vegetable to accompany meat or fish. Or blend in sour cream or yogurt and increase the quantity of spices for a delicious high-protein dip. Use as a sandwich spread with thinly sliced cucumbers and hard-boiled eggs. Or stuff into mushroom caps and broil; serve with a sprinkling of lemon juice.

COOKING DRIED BEANS. The dried beans cook up more quickly than navy or other similar dried beans, and you don't need to soak them overnight. Just simmer for about 40 minutes until tender. Then you can:

- Add to cooked hot white or brown rice with thinly sliced scallions. To make this a main dish for a vegetarian meal, add more vegetables (carrots, peppers, and other vegetables cooked until just crisp-tender).

- Make a bean dinner by simmering in a casserole dish with chopped green onions, salt-pork chunks, a dollop of molasses, and minced green peppers.

- For an Indian flavor, simmer the beans with peeled chunks of raw white potato, a pinch of cumin, cardamom, turmeric, cloves, and ginger, plus carrots and a green vegetable (amaranth or spinach). A few chilis, chopped fine, add heat and make it even more authentic.

Mung Bean

Lu Dou, Luhk Dau

Vigna radiate

(color photo, page xi)

Almost no one grows mung beans in the home garden, but many eat them in the form of bean sprouts. If you buy bean sprouts in the supermarket, they're probably grown from mung beans, since these are regarded as among the finest flavored and are also the easiest to sprout. You can easily grow your own mung beans for sprouting, and you'll have a fine supply of an otherwise impossible-to-obtain vegetable, young mung bean pods.

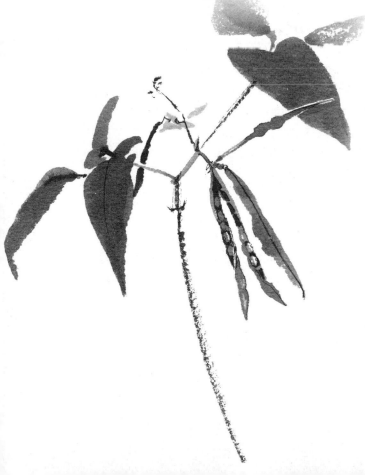

Also called Chinese green beans, mung beans originated in India, where they're known as green gram or golden gram; they are used in innumerable ways in that country. These beans have been cultivated and eaten in Asia, Africa, and Greece for thousands of years. Like all beans, mung beans are high in protein, vitamins, and minerals, making them a deliciously nutritious addition to the diet.

Appearance

Yellow flowers precede the pods, which grow to 3 or 4 inches in length when mature; each pod contains a dozen or so beans.

How to Grow

Getting started. Plant mung beans at the same time as snap beans, when there is no danger of frost and the ground has thoroughly warmed up. In most areas you won't be able to make successive plantings since they require 90 to 120 days to reach maturity.

Sow next to a fence or in a corner of your vegetable garden. The plants are somewhat twining in nature and liable to bother other vegetables if grown too close. If you plant it among corn, it can climb the corn stalks and will mature long after you harvest the last of your corn crop.

Planting. Sow seeds about ½ inch deep. Since plants may grow more than 3 feet high and bush out quite a lot, set the seeds at least 6 to 8 inches apart in rows about 24 inches apart. No thin-ning will be necessary. Seeds germinate in about three days, so you have time to fill in seeds if any failed to come up.

Growing needs. If your garden soil is reasonably good, you don't need to add fertilizer before planting. Mung beans are prolific and grow easily without any special care. Give them the same attention as snap beans and you'll be well rewarded. Provide plenty of moisture and side-dress with compost and a little fertilizer, or diluted fish-and-seaweed fertilizer, when the small yellow flowers start to form pods.

How to Harvest

For fresh beans. To eat mung beans in the pod, gather the immature pods very early, before the seeds have more than barely defined themselves.

For dried beans. To harvest beans for drying, let the pods mature completely and let the plants dry. The pods will curve slightly, and the beans inside will be olive green. (To dry, see the directions on page 74.)

Varieties

Mung beans come green or golden. (The so-called black-seeded mung is a different variety, but it can be used in most of the same ways.) Dates to maturity vary greatly depending on the variety, anywhere from 90 to 120 days.

Allow mung bean vines to twist around your corn stalks.

The basic flavor of mung beans is pleasant and a little bland, so they take on the flavors you add to them and contribute their own interesting texture.

YOUNG PODS. If you harvest the young pods, cook them like snow peas and use in soups, stir-fry dishes, and sukiyaki.

SIMPLY SHELLED. You must remove mature beans from their pods. Once shelled, boil until tender and season lightly with soy sauce and ginger.

PURÉED. The consistency of the beans is slightly sticky, so they lend themselves especially well to bean cakes or a purée. You can also:

- Season the purée with Chinese ingredients.

- Season with garam masala and minced chilis, for an Indian flavor, then simmer or bake for 20 to 30 minutes to allow the flavors to blend.

- The cold purée, appropriately seasoned, makes an excellent high-protein dip for parties. Swirl in a little sour cream or yogurt, garnish with grated carrots, Jerusalem artichokes, or radishes for an attractive addition to a buffet.

SAUCE. For an unusual, high-protein spaghetti sauce, mix cooked or puréed beans with canned tomatoes, tomato paste, oregano, olive oil, basil, minced garlic, and salt to taste. Simmer until the whole is sufficiently thick (at least 1 hour), adding more oil if necessary. To cut down on calories, toss with vegetable spaghetti for a practically starch-free spaghetti dish.

DID YOU KNOW?

In China and Japan, mung beans are used in the manufacture of cellophane noodles. (These noodles are also made from other beans and other ingredients.) In addition, the beans are eaten at every stage from immature pods to dried beans.

ALL ABOUT BEAN SPROUTS

Bean sprouts are only at their best when freshly made — no more than a week or so old. If you like bean sprouts, try growing your beans and sprouting your own crop. Bean sprouts are the easiest and fastest fresh vegetable you can grow, and you can do it in the tiniest kitchen. By sprouting, you can have a fresh vegetable every day of the year.

The most popular sprouted bean in China is the mung, but all beans produce interesting sprouts and each has its own distinctive flavor. The red beans of adzuki sprouts are very noticeable and add visual interest to any dish. Mung beans almost disappear in a forest of white shoots. By utilizing different beans, you can serve and enjoy a rich variety of flavors and textures. Half a cup of this delicious, crunchy vegetable contains only about 16 calories, yet they are higher in protein than most other vegetables and are loaded with vitamins and minerals.

EQUIPMENT NEEDED

A large wide-mouthed jar, colander, or strainer is excellent for sprouting beans. You'll also need several thicknesses of clean cheesecloth or plastic screening to cover the opening. Since the beans need to be rinsed in clear, tepid water two or three times a day, your container should be rigged to make this easy. Use a rubber band to secure two or three thicknesses of cheesecloth over the opening of a wide-mouthed jar, or use a dish towel to cover a colander or strainer. At some kitchen-supply and health-food stores, you can purchase plastic mesh "lids" designed to fit a wide-mouthed canning jar; these are designed just for sprouting and screw on for a tight fit.

Sprout beans in a mason jar fitted with three thicknesses of cheesecloth fastened over the opening with a rubber band.

PREPARING THE BEANS

Wash and pick over the beans to remove any small stones or debris. Use about a ½ cup of dried beans. Once sprouted, these will expand to three to five times their original volume, so if your container won't hold 2½ cups, reduce the amount of dried beans accordingly. If you overcrowd the container, the beans won't sprout as well, and it will be much harder to rinse them well enough to keep them from going mushy.

Soak beans overnight in warm water to cover. (Don't refrigerate.) In the morning, drain the beans in a strainer.

HOW TO SPROUT

Put the drained beans into your container. Fill the container with water, drain, and repeat two or three times to rinse the beans thoroughly. Drain well. Shake the container gently so the beans spread out; if you're using a jar, lay it on its side. Put the container someplace where you won't forget it but it won't be in the way.

There are only two things to do from here on: Rinse the seeds with fresh water and keep them out of the light. Good sprouts are clean, white, and very crisp. Rinsing and draining keeps the seeds moist but not wet and keeps them fresh. Rinse twice a day in cold weather, three or four times a day in hot or very humid weather. Slip the container under the faucet, fill and drain it a couple of times, and put it aside again.

Blocking out the light keeps the sprouts from turning green. Sun or bright light will make them turn green and develop too strong a flavor; white shoots have a more delicate, sweet taste. If you use a clear glass jar, cover it with a couple of dish towels. You can put the jar on a shelf in a closet if you can remember to rinse it. A colander covered with a towel is naturally opaque and can be left on the counter.

Sprouts will gradually fill up the container. After a few crops, you'll be able to estimate more exactly how much you want to eat and what quantity a given container will hold.

Sprouts take three to six days depending on the variety and the temperature of the room. Once they reach the desired size, take them out of the jar and place

(continued on next page)

in a large bowl. Cover with cold water, running your finger through the sprouts to separate them. Remove any bits of hull that float to the surface or any beans that didn't sprout. (There are always a few.) The sprouts are now ready to eat.

To keep the sprouts until dinner or tomorrow's lunch, drain and put in a plastic bag in the refrigerator. For longer storage, put back in the jar and store in the refrigerator. They'll keep for about a week if you rinse them daily.

CULINARY USES

Although any kind of bean sprout can be used in any recipe that calls for sprouts, the taste differs according to the bean used; the only way to determine your preferences is to sprout them all and taste them. There are flavor differences even among varieties of the same beans. Bean sprouts can be eaten raw or cooked, added to your own favorite family recipe, or used in authentic Chinese dishes, such as chow mein.

Salad. For a quick confetti salad, lightly toss bean sprouts with finely chopped carrots and red and green peppers, and dress with rice vinegar and sesame oil. Garnish with a sprinkling of raw or toasted sesame seeds.

Stir-fry. When using bean sprouts in a stir-fry, always add them at the last minute. To make stir-fried beef, toss the beef in a marinade of sherry, soy sauce, a little sugar, and some cornstarch. Then drain and stir-fry for 2 to 3 minutes. Add the vegetables and cook for another minute. Stir in the marinade and cook until thickened. Serve immediately.

When you have bean sprouts handy, you'll find many other occasions to use them. For instance:

- Fill an omelette with bean sprouts that have been stir-fried for a minute.

- A clear consommé looks more inviting with a small handful of sprouts dropped in just before it is served.

- Try a sandwich of bean sprouts, thinly sliced scallions, and a thick spread of cottage cheese instead of butter or mayonnaise.

Yard-Long Bean

CHANG JIANG DOU, DAU GOK

Vigna unguiculata ssp. *sesquipedalis*

(color photo, page xi)

This intriguing bean is related to black-eyed peas as well as to mung beans. It is also called asparagus bean and Chinese long bean. Though everyone agrees its flavor is delicious, descriptions range from like asparagus to not at all like asparagus to similar to snap beans.

The yard-long bean is a pole bean; it needs a support of some sort to climb on. It grows best in very warm weather. Even under ideal conditions, it sometimes won't perform and has a reputation for being an unreliable cropper. When it does bear, it bears heavily. I've had very good luck with it. Try it in your garden; if it works for you, you'll have an unusual addition to your table.

Appearance

This bean grows on a somewhat straggly looking vine that is very aggressive; it's the only vegetable I've grown that can successfully hold its own against spaghetti squash. The flowers are large and very pretty, a combination of white and pale lavender. The pods look like elongated, slender green beans and range from 14 to 18 inches long.

How to Grow

Getting started. Yard-long beans are very, very sensitive to cold, but it can't get too hot for them. In warm climates this is a much easier crop to grow, but with a little care it can be successful in cooler climates, like that of New England. Plant about two weeks later than bush beans; the ground must be truly warm and all thought of frost a dim memory.

Dig in compost and a balanced fertilizer and install poles before planting. Poles should be about 8 feet tall. I use three poles, teepee-fashion, tied together at the top, and let several vines grow up the poles. Arranging them teepee-fashion eliminates the need to set the poles deeply into the ground, and they make an attractive feature in your garden. Leave 4 or 5 feet between teepees. Of course, you can grow them up any support that is convenient for you — fencing, netting, straight poles, or whatever. In that case, allow about 4 inches between plants.

Planting. Sow seeds ½ inch to 1 inch deep. The seeds are quick to germinate in warm soil; you'll see signs of life in 6 to 12 days.

Growing needs. Keep the vines growing briskly with plenty of moisture. Because there is a lot of foliage to feed, side-dressing during the growing season is beneficial. Use compost mixed with a little balanced fertilizer or water in a fish-and-seaweed product, when flowers first appear.

Fasten three bamboo poles near the top, teepee fashion, so that your yard-long bean vines can twine up around them.

How to Harvest

Although plants reach full maturity in 60 to 90 days, you should never wait that long to pick them. Yard-long beans, like snow peas, are at their best when immature, with the bean barely swelling inside the pod and before the pods whiten. The idea is to pick them while the whole pod is still tender enough to be edible, up to 18 inches long. They're so prolific (if they fruit at all) that you'll be hard pressed to keep up with them. Pick and freeze the excess rather than letting them get tough and mature on the vine. Figure on daily picking during the season. If they get ahead of you, shell the mature pods and dry the beans inside.

Varieties

There are two kinds, red-seeded and black-seeded.

Varieties to look for: 3-Feet Plus, Chinese Red Noodle Beans, Canton White Pod.

— CULINARY USES —

You have to cut up yard-long beans no matter how you cook them because a vegetable that's over a foot long is too awkward to deal with otherwise. They cook quickly, which is especially welcome to today's busy cooks. Once prepared you can:

- Use yard-long beans like green beans. Chop into 2-inch lengths, boil briefly, and serve with butter, garnished perhaps with a sprinkling of chopped walnuts or sesame seeds.

- Include them in stir-fry dishes. Combine with shredded pork, sliced mushrooms, burdock, water chestnut, and pak choy leaves and stems.

- Cut smaller pieces for soup and simmer in chicken broth along with a tablespoon of grated lemon rind, a teaspoon of grated fresh ginger, and a few chopped mitsuba leaves.

- For a salad, marinate cooked leftover beans in garlic, lemon juice, soy sauce, and sesame oil.

HOW TO DRY BEANS

Drying is a very satisfactory method of preserving beans. It uses much less energy than freezing, and dried products take up very little space. The goal is to eliminate all moisture to prevent rot and premature germination. It's important not to "cook" the seeds; roasted soybeans are delicious for eating out of hand, but they won't sprout and they won't cook up well. Anything that keeps out moisture makes a suitable container.

Whatever method you use, the racks are very important. They should be as large as possible and must allow maximum air circulation. In an oven, they have to conform to oven size; in the sun, they're limited only by the size you find convenient to handle. You can use window screens, or oven racks covered with screening to keep the beans from falling through. Dehydrators come with their own racks.

PREPARING THE BEANS

Once pods are brown and dry, pull up the whole plant and hang indoors to finish drying. Place something underneath to catch any beans that fall. Once pods split easily, shell and proceed with drying.

DRYING METHODS

Dehydrators. Dehydrators are the easiest way to dry beans. A number of excellent models are available. Most are electric and have removable racks. They're easy to use, take minimal time, and aren't expensive to operate. They come with a fan or blower and a built-in thermostat. Dehydrators eliminate the need to rotate racks or bring them under cover at night. If you grow large quantities of beans, you'll need to dry them in batches, but you won't have to worry about humid spells or rainy weather.

Solar drying. This is the least expensive method, but it won't work in some climates or during periods of humid weather. You need a spell of long, clear, dry sunny days, and a spot in full sun to place your racks. Since you'll be drying at different times depending on when your beans mature, everything depends on the spell of weather at the time you're ready to dry. Plant material won't wait for a dry spell, so it's best to have an alternative plan available.

If you have very changeable weather, use oven racks for solar drying. Whenever a shower threatens or a day turns muggy, move the racks to the oven to continue drying without interruption. It's important to dry steadily; intermittent damp and dry conditions will invariably cause your beans to mold or rot.

Note: No matter how dry and clear the weather, be sure to take your racks in at night. The night air is always moister and there's often a heavy dew even during a very dry spell.

Cover beans drying outdoors with a single layer of cheesecloth. This keeps them from being blown off the racks by the wind and keeps them free from insects. It also deters birds. Secure the cheesecloth so it doesn't flap around or blow away. You can run an elastic thread around the edges of the cheesecloth to hold it snugly in place. Or thread ordinary string in the same fashion, leaving two loose string ends to draw together and tie in a loose bow. The cheesecloth is easy to wash, dry, and store to reuse year after year.

Attic drying. A nice hot but airy attic works well because you don't need to bring in trays at night. Mine works for herbs but it is not airy enough for beans (aside from the fact that it's too stuffed with accumulated stuff). If you have the attic and the room, it might be worth investing in a good attic fan for this purpose. This only works if your spot in the attic is easily accessible; if you don't check on your beans often enough the whole crop may be ruined through neglect.

Oven drying. Oven drying is much quicker than solar drying; it shouldn't take more than 6 to 8 hours altogether. Use oven racks prepared as described on the previous page, but omit the cheesecloth covers. Preheat your oven before putting in the beans. Set the oven very low — 140°F — or you'll roast the beans rather than dry them. Check your oven thermostat with a portable oven thermometer.

About once an hour, rotate the position of your racks. Simply move them all down one level and put the bottom rack on top. If possible, the beans should be close but not touching. If this is too tedious, shake the racks slightly when you rotate them to shift the beans and expose different surfaces.

(continued on next page)

To assure good ventilation and eliminate moisture, prop the oven door open slightly while drying. Turn on the ventilator fan over the stove; it will increase air circulation, especially if an open window is nearby.

STORING THE BEANS

Test a few beans to make sure they're really dry by placing them on a hard surface and hitting with a hammer. If they shatter, they're ready for storage; if they mash instead, give them more drying time.

After removing the beans from the sun or dryer, let them cool *completely* before putting them away. Do this in a dry place so they don't reabsorb the moisture you've just driven off.

Once dried and cooled, put in tightly sealed containers (a plastic bag, for instance) and store in a cool (50°F), dry place out of sunlight. To kill any insect larvae, place thoroughly dry beans in the freezer for a few days before moving them to their storage spot.

It's a good idea to check each batch for the first couple of weeks. If you see any moisture forming on the inside of the container, dry for another couple of hours, preferably in the oven, and put into new containers. Discard any beans that develop mold.

Flowering Kale

Wu Tou Gan Lan, Hwa Choy

Brassica oleracea Acephala Group

(color photo, page xii)

This vegetable is so beautiful that many gardeners grow it as an ornamental, never knowing it is edible. If you wonder why you haven't noticed it in seed catalogs, it may be because you've been looking at vegetables and it's in the flower section. Only recently has flowering kale come out of hiding among the annuals and perennials and been admitted to the suddenly fashionable company of edibles.

Appearance

The ornamental feature of flowering kale (or flowering cabbage) — aside from its perfect shape — is the spectacular range of colors the foliage turns upon exposure to cold weather. Individual plants look like huge cabbage roses and come in striking combinations of red, pink, and green.

How to Grow

Getting started. It seems a waste to plant flowering kale in the vegetable garden, so I usually reserve it for a container or bed that is otherwise full of flowers and herbs. It makes an excellent bedding plant because it stays nicely within bounds, and it's neat and precise looking.

4

THE CHINESE CABBAGES

FLOWERING KALE • CHINESE BROCCOLI •
PAK CHOY • CHINESE CABBAGE

I've called this chapter "The Chinese Cabbages" to point out the fact
that there are so many different kinds. As a group, they are one of our
most ancient vegetables. Botanists can't determine where Chinese
cabbages originated because they've been cultivated for thousands
of years and are now found from Newfoundland to southern China.
Celts may have brought them to the British Isles, but they were grown
in Asia long before that time. Some of the early varieties grown in the
United States (where it's been cultivated since 1900) came from Germany or Holland. In recent years, new varieties have been coming in
from Japan and China, so now you can see more types of Chinese cabbages in your local supermarket and farmer's markets.

Almost every vegetable catalog offers at least one Chinese cabbage variety, but it's worth sending for catalogs that offer more of a
selection. Read the descriptions carefully; sometimes the cabbages
and mustards are hard to tell apart The heading types are the true
Chinese cabbages, *Brassica rapa* Pekinensis Group. The leafy types are
Chinese mustard, *B. juncea* (see page 11). In addition, flowering kale
is a colorful vegetable most often grown purely as an ornamental.
Finally, Chinese broccoli is similar to our more familiar broccoli but
different enough to be worth space in your garden.

Planting. Sow seeds in rich loamy soil ½ inch deep and 8 to 10 inches apart, in rows 16 inches apart. If you want to start your seeds in flats, these seedlings transplant easily; just disturb them as little as possible when moving into the open garden.

Growing needs. Ornamental flowering kales grow like common cabbages. Because they're smaller you can plant them close together for a breathtaking display. Give them plenty of moisture and fertilize every four weeks with a fish-and-seaweed or balanced fertilizer.

Flowering kale develops on thick stalks above the ground. Hill up the soil so the head rests on it; otherwise it may topple over and break. If spaced so closely that plants support one another at maturity, this may not be necessary.

Pest potential. Flowering kale doesn't seem to entice pests and diseases, except for the green cabbageworm, the larval form of the white cabbage butterfly. Their camouflage is almost perfect, so look carefully and hand-pick whenever you see them — even the tiny ones. Or dust plants with the biological insecticide *Bacillus thuringiensis* (Bt).

How to Harvest

Pick the kale anytime you want after plants have formed loose heads, as early as 55 days. To enjoy their color, leave plants to the point of complete maturity, but use them as soon as possible after you pick them or store in a refrigerator or cool cellar. They do not keep as well as other cabbages.

Varieties

Almost every catalog lists it somewhere, often called "ornamental kale" or "ornamental cabbage."

— CULINARY USES —

Use flowering kale like any other kale or cabbage. Shred it, boil it, bake it, stuff it! Miniatures also make beautiful, unusual centerpieces, alone or combined with other flowers. Tuck curly parsley or miniture yellow marigolds among the leaves of the green-and-white varieties.

For a show-stopper buffet salad, break up the head, scald leaves briefly, then reform into the original shape (in a bowl). Then stuff shrimp salad between the leaves. Beautiful!

Chinese Broccoli

JIE LAN, GAI LAN

Brassica oleracea Alboglabra Group

(color photo, page xii)

*I*f you're always in a hurry, you'll welcome this delicious, quick-cooking vegetable in your garden and kitchen. Chinese broccoli cooks up like ordinary broccoli, but it's even easier to prepare. It's eaten stems and all, like the European broccoli rabe. Just to confuse things, it's sometimes called Chinese kale despite its resemblance to broccoli. It is also sometimes called white flowering broccoli.

Broccoli is one of the oldest of the Brassicas. It was eaten in ancient Greece over 2,000 years ago. It's still enjoyed today both in the simplest cottage and the fanciest restaurant. It's good hot or cold, and the florets can be used as crudités with a spicy dip.

Since it's quick and easy to prepare and versatile, you might want to give over a good-sized patch to this valuable vegetable. It won't limit your garden because it's a two-season crop — spring and fall — which allows you to grow a different crop in that same spot during the summer months.

Appearance

Chinese broccoli looks like regular broccoli that didn't quite make it to maturity or was picked too soon by an impatient gardener. The stems are long in proportion to the flowers, and the heads are much smaller than those we are used to. The flowers are white and larger than regular broccoli, though not so numerous.

How to Grow

Getting started. As a cool-season plant, Chinese broccoli goes into the ground either in early spring for a late-spring crop or toward the end of summer for a late-fall crop. Plant short-season, warmth-loving vegetables in the same spot between broccoli crops. Figure on 14 days for germination of the seed.

Planting. Sow seeds ½ inch deep and 1 inch apart in rows 12 inches apart. Thin seedlings to stand 6 inches apart when they are 3 to 4 inches tall. Cooked very quickly, the thinnings are a gardener's secret vegetable. Only a little butter and salt should be used for this delicate dish.

Growing needs. Chinese broccoli matures quickly without much attention. Fertilize lightly after the first three weeks, more heavily when the buds begin to form. What broccoli needs most is plenty of water.

How to Harvest

Like regular broccoli, the flavor of Chinese broccoli is best just before the flowers open. Pick the center buds first to encourage formation of side shoots, giving you a second and third harvest. Always include a long stub on the stem when you cut the flowering stalk. Once you've picked it, the flowers may open slightly, but this won't spoil the flavor. Continue harvesting as long as the plant produces new buds.

Varieties

Varieties to look for: Thick Stem Winner, Blue Star, Hybrid Blue Wonder.

DID YOU KNOW?

Chinese broccoli is very nutritious. It's a good source of vitamins C and A, as well as calcium, iron, and other minerals.

Although regular broccoli is frequently substituted in Chinese dishes, the cook who wants an authentic Chinese flavor would never be satisfied with that substitution. It's the subtle differences that make life interesting, and the difference between the flavors of Chinese and regular broccoli is substantial enough to be worth fussing about.

Chinese cooks usually peel the stems as well as split the thicker ones partway; stems prepared this way will cook faster and can be added to stir-fry dishes with just a minute or two to cook. I don't have the time for extra preparation, so I pick my broccoli when it's a little younger so I don't have to peel it, but I do split the thicker stems.

TRADITIONAL CHINESE-STYLE. To prepare Chinese broccoli in one of its commonest Chinese forms, cut the broccoli into 2-inch pieces and stir-fry for 1 minute. Add a little water, cover, and cook the broccoli for 2 more minutes. Add oyster sauce to the oil-and-water liquid in the pan, stir until heated, and serve the broccoli with the sauce spooned over it. Or add minced garlic to the first step, and use chicken broth and a little soy sauce instead of the water. Thicken with cornstarch if desired.

WITH HOLLANDAISE SAUCE. For a pleasant surprise, serve Chinese broccoli with hollandaise sauce. You'll assume you're eating regular broccoli until you taste it.

STIR-FRIED OR STEAMED. Chinese broccoli is good stir-fried with beef, mushrooms, and water chestnuts, plus freshly grated ginger and soy sauce. It also holds up well to steaming.

SUKIYAKI AND TEMPURA. If you make sukiyaki, Chinese broccoli florets, dipped in tempura batter and deep fried, are especially delicious.

SALAD. Any leftover Chinese broccoli makes a good cold salad with a vinaigrette dressing. Don't add the dressing until you're ready to serve or the cooked leaves and florets will get mushy. If you've used just the leaves and florets and saved the cooked stems, marinate these in a spicy dressing for an hour or so and serve as a kind of pickle. Stems for this use should be just crisp-tender.

Pak Choy

Bai Cai, Bok Choy

Brassica rapa Chinensis Group

(color photo, page xii)

Pak choy is closely related to Chinese mustard greens (see page 11). The former was sometimes called Chinese white mustard cabbage, the latter Chinese green mustard cabbage. Pak choy doesn't look anything like the Chinese cabbages we've been talking about up to this point. You've seen it in your supermarket and you've eaten part of it (the green leaves, not the white ribs) in won ton soup in Chinese restaurants. The green leafy vegetable in Chinese dishes is usually pak choy — and so are the white, crisp, inch-long pieces you find in combination with it.

Pak choy is rich in vitamin C and minerals and is a good source of dietary fiber. It's very popular throughout Europe, especially in France, where it has been cultivated since the 1800s.

Appearance

Pak choy is an attractive vegetable. The large leaves are a beautiful, glossy dark green, the ribs a bright white. It doesn't form a tight head and doesn't look like either a regular cabbage or a Chinese cabbage; it is more similar to Swiss chard.

The blanched hearts are considered a particular delicacy, and Chinese produce stores put a premium price on them. Pak choy is often sold with its little bright yellow flowers nestled in the center; unlike common broccoli, this is a desirable stage to eat. In your own garden, you can enjoy both the blanched hearts and the flowers without having to pay high prices for them.

How to Grow

Getting started. Pak choy is a cool-weather vegetable. Plant in early spring or the middle of August in cool climates, and as early as March or as late as September in warmer regions. You can extend the fall crop by harvesting the outer leaves and allowing the rest of the plant to continue growing. The spring season isn't long enough for this treatment, however, so pick the whole plant while still small. Then, if a spell of unseasonably warm weather should occur, pick the entire crop right away or you will lose it.

Planting. Sow seeds ¼ inch deep and about 2 inches apart, in rows 18 inches apart. When the plants are about 4 inches high, thin to stand about 6 inches apart. The thinnings make good eating.

Growing needs. Like all cabbages, pak choy should be encouraged to grow briskly, and the best way to accomplish this is with regular watering. In the spring, nature often takes care of that for you. Mulch to keep the soil cool, and plants will come through occasional hot spells without any problems.

A rich loamy soil gives you the best crop. A little fertilizer and compost mixed in with the soil before planting is good if you don't overdo it; pak choy does better with frequent light feedings rather than less-frequent heavy feedings. Fertilize lightly every two weeks and give a side-dressing of compost when the plants are six weeks old.

DRIED GREENS

Here's an interesting way to preserve excess pak choy: Make "Choy Gone." Wash and separate each leaf, parboil for 5 minutes or until the color changes, drain, separate each leaf, and dry in the sun. Soak leaves about 2 hours before using, and simmer until tender.

This is a very popular Asian way of using this vegetable; travelers bring back snapshots of lines of pak choy hung out to dry like some strange kind of washing. If you don't have a clothesline, it's worth rigging up one for this. You can do it just as easily on an apartment rooftop as in a backyard.

Pick the outside, mature leaves of a pak choy plant.

How to Harvest

Pak choy matures fairly quickly — in about eight weeks — but you don't have to wait until maturity to enjoy it. In the late summer and fall, gather mature outside leaves; as long as you don't disturb the heart, the plant will continue to produce more leaves. I don't recommend this procedure in the spring.

Varieties

Pak choy is a mustard and is often found under that heading. Also search under Chinese cabbage, Asian greens, or Asian vegetables.

Varieties to look for: Long White Petiole, Short White Petiole, Canton Choice.

— CULINARY USES —

Pak choy is two vegetables in one: the leaves cook up like spinach, the ribs like asparagus. If using both in a stir-fry wok dish, put the ribs (cut into 1 inch lengths) in first for a minute or two, then add the leaves (cut into large pieces) for just a minute. It is also good in chop suey and similar dishes.

IN SOUPS. The leaves are also used as a last-minute addition to soup, simmered just long enough to go slightly limp. The first outside leaves of really mature plants should either be discarded or reserved for making a vegetable stock.

AS A SIDE DISH. To cook as a side dish (with roast chicken for example), separate the leaves from the ribs, cut the ribs into 1-inch pieces, and simmer for 5 minutes in boiling salted water. Then add the leaves, torn into large pieces, and cook for 3 minutes more. Drain well and serve with melted butter and a sprinkling of minced fresh cilantro.

Chinese Cabbage

Huan Ya Bai, Wong Nga Pak

Brassica rapa Pekinensis Group

(color photo, page xii)

This is known as a heading cabbage for the obvious reason that it forms a fairly tight, compact head on maturity. It's not round like regular cabbage but tall like romaine lettuce. It is known by many names: napa cabbage, hakusai, Tianjin cabbage, michihili, and Chinese celery cabbage.

Appearance

The Chinese cabbages most commonly found in supermarkets are the michihili and napa types. Michihili types are tall, about a foot or so, and more like romaine lettuce. Napa types are shorter and chunky-looking, about 8 inches thick and a bit taller than wide. Both are mild flavored and deliciously crisp with pale green leaves, usually attractively crinkled, and sometimes shading to darker green.

How to Grow

Getting started. Chinese cabbage is a cool-weather crop that prefers short days. For foolproof crops, plant in midsummer for a fall crop.

For spring planting, use a bolt-resistant variety and start seeds indoors four to five weeks before the last frost. (See page 201.) If you sow seeds outdoors, wait until after the last expected frost date to minimize the risk of bolting. Or take a chance and plant outdoors at the same time you plant your lettuce. Seedlings grow well in the cool temperatures, but if you have a cold spell, they may go to seed before forming a head.

When transplanting seedlings started indoors, take care to avoid disturbing the roots and to shock the seedlings as little as possible. Whatever you can do to fool your seedlings into not knowing they're being transplanted improves your chances of success. Set plants 14 to 24 inches apart (follow the spacing recommended for the specific variety).

Planting. For fall crops, plant seeds outdoors three months before the first frost date in your area. Sow the seeds ½ inch deep and with about 1 inch between them. When the seedlings have four true leaves and are about 4 inches high, thin the plants to 18 inches apart in rows 18 to 30 inches apart. Eat the thinnings; they're a special treat.

Growing needs. Chinese cabbage grows well just about everywhere in the United States. An ordinary loamy vegetable garden soil does fine if you dig in some compost and a balanced fertilizer before planting. If your soil is acidic, be sure to add lime, since this vegetable will not be happy in an acidic soil.

Always add lime at least two weeks before sowing. Side-dress with more compost plus a little fertilizer when seedlings are about 4 inches high, and again every five weeks to keep the plants growing rapidly. Chinese cabbage likes a lot of moisture, so keep it well watered between rains.

Pest potential. Chinese cabbage is more resistant to pests and diseases than regular cabbage. In general cabbageworms and other cabbage pests will pass this by.

How to Harvest

Varieties differ greatly in days to maturity. Harvest when the heads are firm and appear fully developed.

Though heat sensitive, Chinese cabbage tolerates quite cold weather when mature. Harvest it before a heavy frost, but don't worry if a light frost should creep up on you; it won't spoil your crop. Once temperatures drop below 50°F, the plants stop growing, but they stand well and you don't have to pick them immediately.

Once harvested, Chinese cabbages store well. They keep for two to three months in a cool cellar or refrigerator. Keep an eye on them, and if they seem to be getting less fresh-looking, pickle whatever is left. You can also freeze Chinese cabbage.

Varieties

The two types available in most catalogs are the michihli and napa types described on page 86. Several varieties of each are available. Some are recommended for spring crops (these may be described as "bolt resistant"), others for fall. All spring cabbages can be sown for a fall harvest, but fall cabbages sown in the spring tend to bolt. For winter storage, fall varieties are better.

Varieties to look for: Hybrid Super, Hybrid Hwa King WR60, Michihili.

— CULINARY USES —

Use Chinese cabbage any way you use ordinary cabbage. The flavor is more delicate than cabbage. If you grow Chinese cabbage, you'll be delighted with its versatility and will want to try all these different ways:

SALAD. It makes a truly delicious and unusual coleslaw: Shred it finely and toss with ginger, soy sauce, Asian sesame oil, and rice wine vinegar. The Chinese would add a little sugar, but that's optional.

STIR-FRY. In stir-fried dishes, add as one of the last ingredients so the cooking time is especially brief and its natural crispness is retained.

PICKLING. In Asia it is much favored for pickling, and the result is both similar to and different from our sauerkraut.

5

A CHINESE VEGETABLE POTPOURRI

BURDOCK • DAYLILY • SNOW PEA • ASPARAGUS PEA
• CHINESE RADISH • CHINESE EGGPLANT

By dictionary definition, a potpourri is a miscellaneous collection. This chapter contains the Chinese vegetables that don't fit into the other groups. Some of these vegetables are familiar, so you'll find it all the more interesting to discover what the Chinese varieties are like. You can grow them happily side by side with the old familiar varieties and have East meet West right in your own garden and kitchen.

Burdock

NGAO PONG, NIU PANG

Arctium lappa

(color photo, page xiii)

If you think of burdock as that bothersome weed with the prickly burrs, you may wonder what it's doing in a book on Chinese vegetables. As a vegetable, you may be more familiar with it by its Japanese name, gobo. As gobo, it is an important and much enjoyed Japanese vegetable, lending itself to a number of classic dishes.

Many people don't realize that *gobo* is burdock and eat it with relish in Asian restaurants thinking it's some unobtainable exotic ingredient. Actually, burdock is so easy to grow in the United States that it grows wild almost everywhere. Burdock is not native to North America, though like many other immigrants, it has thrived here. It was introduced by the early settlers and is also known as edible burdock.

Appearance

Burdock looks very much like the wild burdock that grows in much of the United States. It's a tall plant, growing up to 8 feet under ideal conditions. The flowers are purple and numerous but comparatively inconspicuous, quickly turning into burrs if allowed to go to seed. The slender, carrot- or parsnip-shaped roots can grow as long as 4 feet.

Most of the time they will grow about 24 inches long. They are brown with white flesh.

How to Grow

Getting started. The mature roots are ready about two and a half months after planting, so an early-spring planting will give you a fall crop. If allowed to winter over, burdock (like Jerusalem artichokes) will be one of your earliest root crops. You can also plant in late fall for spring use. Burdock roots grow best in average, sandy loam with a pH near neutral. Dig deep, down to at least 24 inches, when preparing the soil to accommodate the long roots. Incorporate compost and a balanced fertilizer (ideally one such as 4-6-6 in which the first number — nitrogen — is lower than the other two). Avoid high-nitrogen fertilizers, which promote leafy growth, since burdock is grown primarily for its roots.

Planting. Although the plant is very hardy and winters over almost everywhere, the seeds need warmth for germination. To speed germination, soak seeds in fairly warm water and leave in a warm place overnight. The next day, drain and sow immediately. Sow seeds ½ to 1 inch deep, about 6 inches apart and in rows 20 inches apart.

Growing needs. Mulch so you aren't tempted to overwater, which would give you good top growth but keep the roots smaller than ideal. Keep the flowers picked off so the plant doesn't go to seed. You don't want this vegetable reverting to its wild state.

Pest potential. Pests and diseases don't trouble this plant much. If your area has nematodes, plant marigolds thickly through your vegetable garden and plow under in the fall when preparing the soil for winter.

DID YOU KNOW?

Like Jerusalem artichokes, burdock roots are very high in inulin (a polysaccharide). The dry weight of inulin in a mature root can run as high as 45. Since inulin is acceptable in diabetic diets, this is a welcome addition to the menu for those who are limited in the carbohydrates they can eat.

The root has diuretic properties and has therefore been used in the treatment of some kidney diseases. Its somewhat pungent flavor and availability in early spring make it inevitable that people have esteemed it as a "blood purifier" or tonic. Since it is rich in iron and zinc and supplies smaller quantities of several vitamins and minerals, its reputation as a tonic may have some merit.

How to Harvest

For immature plants. Gather young leaves and young shoots in the spring. For a special treat, gather the young shoots with their tiny roots attached; cook the two together like baby beets with greens.

For roots. To harvest the roots, dig deeply with a spading fork until a gentle tug frees the loosened root. If you've succeeded in growing extra-long roots, you may have to dig a trench next to them to get at them. Roots 2 to 3 feet long are the most manageable, so aim for that size.

If you leave the plant undisturbed and don't harvest the root, burdock will die down over the winter and come up again each season. There isn't much point to letting it do this as the roots are best the first year. Treat it like an annual and plant from seeds each season.

Varieties

There are two species: *Arctium lappa* and *A. minus*. The one you find growing wild throughout much of the United States is the smaller *A. minus*; it is hardly comparable to the aristocratic, cultivated *A. lappa*. Don't buy any seeds other than *A. lappa*. The most popular variety is 'Takinogawa Long'. 'Watanabe' is a shorter variety for those with clay or shallow soil. You may need to look under "gobo" as well as under "burdock" to find seeds.

DID YOU KNOW?

Wild American burdock, which can be a nuisance weed, is very bitter. Although, like the Chinese vegetable *Arctium lappa*, the wild burdock is edible, it must be parboiled to remove the bitterness.

Burdock is enjoyed as a vegetable in many countries, but it reaches its culinary peak in Japan and China. While the young leaves and stems are edible — prepared like spinach and asparagus, respectively — the most important part of the plant is the long, slender root. The flavor of burdock varies somewhat, depending on the conditions under which it's grown and when the root is harvested. To me, the flavor is sweetly pungent and agreeable. The texture is crisp when raw and retains this quality if used in stir-fry dishes. Unlike wild American burdock, burdock can be cooked along with carrots and other root vegetables to make a richly flavored stew.

YOUNG ROOTS, RAW. When very young, the roots can be gathered, peeled, and eaten out of hand like a radish, perhaps with a salt shaker handy.

MATURE ROOTS, COOKED. The mature root should be peeled, soaked for 5 to 10 minutes in salted water or parboiled for 3 minutes (to get rid of the slight bitterness), then cooked any way you please. Many recipes don't call for scalding before cooking, so you can try omitting this step and see if the results are satisfactory. You may not feel it is worth the trouble. Here are some common ways of preparing it:

- As an interesting addition to baked beans of all kinds.

- Use it to add character to a bland broth.

- Blanch, cool, and shred, then cook in butter for about 10 minutes, then combine with 2 tablespoons of vinegar and cook, covered, for another 10 minutes over low heat; sprinkle with parsley and serve hot.

PICKLED. In Japan, both the stems and the roots are pickled. You can buy pickled burdock roots in an Asian grocery store if you want to taste them before making your own. Somehow the pickling seems to make the taste hotter, so you end up with an agreeably spicy condiment that does wonders for a platter of cold meats on a hot summer day.

Daylily

JIN ZHEN CAI, GUM JUM

Hemerocallis fulva

(color photo, page xiii)

The daylily owes its name to flowers that last only for a single day. The plants bloom so profusely that many people don't realize this. These plants produce an enormous number of buds, and the Chinese (who never waste anything edible) eat daylily buds fresh and dry them for a special out-of-season treat.

Daylilies are native to Asia, even though in many parts of the eastern United States the countryside lights up with these beautiful flowers in summer. Daylilies have acclimated themselves so successfully that they form large masses wherever they're allowed to grow. Since they tolerate almost any soil and grow in many parts of the United States, you probably know someone who has them on his or her property. If so, transplant some to your own property or terrace.

Once planted, a bed of daylilies will increase each year. No matter how many you eat, there will soon be more than you can use. The clumps can be easily divided to be planted elsewhere.

Appearance

Daylilies grow from fleshy, tuberous roots and form clumps of slender, straplike leaves. The cheery flowers are funnel-shaped, and stiff stalks hold them well above the clumps. The flowers of the common daylily (also called the tawny daylily and tiger lily) are burnt orange and grow on stems up to 3 feet tall, though the foliage clumps are only about 2 feet tall.

How to Grow

Getting started. If you don't know someone who has daylilies, it's worth checking with a local garden club. Anyone who has them will have enough to share. Otherwise, you may need to order them if you want the common species. Every nursery sells potted daylilies, but they'll be a newer variety. If you order from a catalog, you'll tend to get them either in the spring or fall. If you dig them from a friend's yard, you can take them anytime, but they're easiest to handle in the spring when the shoots are about 3 inches high. They aren't fussy about being moved; you can even transplant daylilies when they're blooming, as long as you water them in well.

Planting. As long as they're not in full shade or don't have wet feet, you can put daylilies anywhere and they'll reward you with abundant blooms.

You can naturalize daylilies, put them toward the back of a flower bed, or give them their own bed. The fleshy roots should be set at the same level as they were growing, with the crown (where roots meet shoots) just below soil level.

Growing needs. Dig in some compost before planting, and water well after planting. Once established, your daylilies won't need any watering. A little admiration occasionally is a good thing for a person, pet, or plant; otherwise daylilies require no care. The common daylily dislikes rich soil, and the clumps don't need dividing more than

Plant daylilies so that the fleshy roots are set just below soil level.

every five years or so. Even then, you don't *have* to divide them, but you'll get even more handsome plants if you do. Modern long-blooming daylily varieties such as 'Happy Returns' and the ubiquitous 'Stella d'Oro' need supplemental feeding to keep up their impressive show, but species and older varieties don't. Some compost every year or two is beneficial but not essential.

How to Harvest

Pick the buds when they're plump but before they open — that's all. The fleshy roots and young leaves of daylilies are also eaten in Asia. But with so many other things to try, I've never gotten around to them. If you're adventurous, you can try out a recipe if you come upon one that appeals to you.

Varieties

The common daylily (*Hemerocallis fulva*) and the tiger lily (*Lilium lancifolium,* formerly *L. tigrinum*) are the lilies most commonly found growing wild in the countryside. Some people confuse the two, but tiger lilies are true lilies with several spotted orange flowers dangling from each 4- to 6-foot-tall stalk. These two species are the most traditional lilies for the kitchen. There are many Chinese and Japanese varieties of daylily. If you choose early, midsummer, and late varieties, you can have lilies in bloom from spring to late summer.

DID YOU KNOW?

Daylilies thrive equally well in city or country, wherever you choose to put them. They're so decorative, and they cheer up the dry, hot days of summer when it's hard going for other flowers. They're perennial, so put them in a corner of the yard or the flower garden rather than the vegetable garden where you'll have to work around them. They don't need the regular care and attention that vegetables usually require and thrive more on neglect than on coddling.

The most esteemed part of the daylily is the bud. Since daylilies bloom for a day, you'll always have a fresh crop to pick and can serve them as often as you like. You can gather buds over a long period without harming plants. There seem to be more recipes for dried than for fresh buds, but once you're become accustomed to cooking them, you may find yourself making up new dishes for both forms.

GOLDEN NEEDLES. The Chinese call dried lily buds "golden needles," an ingredient you'll see in many Chinese dishes. In the market, golden needles are usually offered in the form of a pressed, golden block that's cut to provide the number of ounces you require. If you prepare golden needles from your own garden, store the dried buds (without pressing) in any container that will keep out moisture. They are 2 to 3 inches long.

Once dried, the buds will keep a long time. To use, soak in warm water for about 30 minutes. Squeeze dry, and cut into lengths the size of the meat and vegetables in your dish. (All ingredients in Chinese cooking are traditionally cut into similar sizes, small enough to be eaten with chopsticks without needing a knife.) The harder bits of stem should be snapped off before the buds are added to a dish. Dried lily buds are very nutritious.

CHINESE-STYLE. A typical Chinese dish combines mushrooms, shredded pork, scallions, and water chestnuts with (soaked) dried daylily buds. Start by stir-frying the foods that require longer cooking, and add the others one by one. Finally, add soy sauce, cornstarch, sugar, and a little sesame oil for flavoring along with a small amount of chicken broth or other liquid. Cover and simmer for 2 to 3 minutes. Serve with rice.

JAPANESE-STYLE. Cook the fresh buds tempura-style.

Snow Pea

SHID DOU, HO LAN DOU

Pisum sativum var. *macrocarpon*

(color photo, page xiii)

Since I discovered snow peas (sometimes called edible-podded peas), I don't think I'll ever again bother growing garden (English) peas. The chief reason I prefer snow peas is the yield. Once you've shelled a bowl of garden peas, you have a great pile of pods for the compost heap and a small handful of peas for dinner. A bowlful of snow peas, on the other hand, gives you a bowlful for dinner. No tedious shelling, no waste. You eat pods and all and they're sweet, crisp, and meaty.

Snow peas are expensive to buy, but they're so easy to grow. And even a small patch can feed a family of four. They're a worthwhile addition to your vegetable garden in every way, good eating and also beautiful, actually showy, when in flower.

People unfamiliar with snow peas sometimes think I'm growing sweet peas and stop to ask me how I do it in this area. (Sweet peas don't do well in my part of Connecticut.) The flowers don't come in all the colors of sweet peas and don't grow in the same profusion, but they have the lovely, pastel violet lavender and the same general appearance of a true sweet pea. They're attractive enough to grow — as I do — in the front of the house and pretty enough to use as a cut flower.

Appearance

Snow peas look like garden peas except for the color and size of the flowers; the shape of the leaves and flowers is much the same. Not all snow pea flowers are lavender; some varieties are snow white. Some catalogs describe my violet-lavender flowers as "red" or "reddish," which hardly does them justice. If you have a choice, pick a lavender-flowered variety for a feast for the eyes as well as the palate. Most varieties are described as growing about 2½ to 3 feet tall, but in practice many will grow taller.

How to Grow

Getting started. Sow snow peas where they are to grow as early in the spring as the ground can be worked. They don't mind cold, wet ground and can be seeded as much as six weeks before the date of your last killing frost.

They grow poorly in the heat of midsummer but can be planted again for a fall crop. For the fall crop, sow from August to mid-September in cooler climates (check the days to maturity and count backward from the date of your first killing frost). In mild climates, they can be sown in October or even later and grown throughout the winter for a spring harvest. The first light frosts won't bother them a bit. If you have a warm spot (like the side of my garage) and some luck, you can get a crop surprisingly late in the fall.

Planting. The best way to plant snow peas (or any peas, for that matter) is in a 6-inch-deep trench. The plants grow better if earth is pushed up to cover the first few inches of stems as the plants grow taller. This is much easier to achieve by filling in a trench than by hilling up from the surface of the soil. Sowing in a trench makes watering more efficient and keeps the roots in the cooler, moist soil below the surface.

Dig your trench 8 to 10 inches deep and incorporate a balanced fertilizer into the soil. Also check the soil pH, which should range between 6.0 and 7.0. If yours is more acidic, incorporate limestone at least two weeks before

DID YOU KNOW?

Snow peas are a good source of vitamin C, vitamin A, some B vitamins, and iron. They also contain vitamin K, protein, and dietary fiber. Their caloric content is about half that of garden peas if you compare by weight; because they're so much bulkier, a 1-cup serving of snow peas has only a quarter of the calories of 1 cup of garden peas.

sowing. If you've never grown peas or beans before, treating seeds or soil with an inoculant improves yields by supplying the bacteria needed for nitrogen fixation. (Inoculants are available from seed suppliers; check label directions to see whether to add to seeds or soil.) Cover this fertilizer-enriched soil with plain soil in which to set your seeds.

Sow thickly and ½ to 1 inch deep, since germination rates are sometimes low. If seeds germinate well, thin to about 2 inches apart. I find peas don't mind being crowded if you keep them well watered.

Growing needs. Vines grow from 16 to 60 inches or more, so plan your supports accordingly. You can't always count on dwarf varieties bushing. I grew one described as "dwarf, needing no support." Well, maybe. Mine grew 5-foot-high vines, but they were absolutely delicious. This sometimes happens with the so-called dwarf varieties, so prepare to put up a support if your bushes take off and start vining.

When the plants are 8 inches high, fill in the trench to almost soil level; leaving it a little below soil level makes thorough watering easier. Keep the soil on the moist side at all times. Mulch is especially beneficial for peas; it keeps the soil moist, and it keeps it cool, which is equally important. Don't let the mulch actually touch the vines, or it will rot them. Before mulching, lay down an inch of wood ashes, if you have them. During the growing season, side-dress with a little balanced fertilizer or feed with a fish-and-seaweed product.

SNOW PEA BONUS

The bonus is not for you — at least not right away — but for your garden. Since snow peas are nitrogen-fixing plants, use the dried vines and roots as a nitrogen-rich mulch and till them under at the end of the season. I think they're wasted on the compost heap and should be returned to your garden soil at the earliest opportunity. If you don't till your soil at the end of the season, cut vines off at soil level to let roots decompose in place and use the tops as mulch. This is an easy and organic way to enrich your soil with nitrogen.

How to Harvest

The peas form quickly and in tremendous quantity; I've never known a more prolific vegetable. It's important to pick pods while they're still immature. If you let any go to seed, the vine will stop producing. It's hard not to overlook some. My husband, Don, taught me to shake the vine gently. This makes the peas swing back and forth, and the movement makes the pods easy to spot. Now I never miss a pod.

At the height of the season you may have to pick your snow peas twice a day. This sounds incredible to anyone who hasn't grown snow peas, but it's no exaggeration. I end up with pounds in my refrigerator and usually have to take off a morning to freeze a batch.

Varieties

Unlike many Asian vegetables, with snow peas you have more of a selection. Some varieties are dwarf and have a bushy rather than a vining habit.

Generally speaking, the bush varieties bear earlier than the vine varieties. I've grown only the vining kind, but the bush varieties theoretically don't have to be supported. If you grow the tall varieties up the side of a fence the way I do, vines are less work than bush types; they grow by themselves with only an occasional assist if the winds are from the wrong direction, and they're easier to harvest.

Varieties to look for: Mammoth Melting Sugar, Oregon Sugar Pod II, Premium.

— CULINARY USES —

Snow peas combine the best features of snap beans (tender and crisp) and garden peas (sweet and meaty). They can be used any way you would use either of the other vegetables. They are, of course, essential to Asian cuisine and are used in soups, meat dishes, stir-fry dishes, and sukiyaki. If you have vegetarian friends who won't eat shrimp tempura, give them snow peas tempura as a special treat.

Snow peas go with fish and combine well with other vegetables. Especially useful for busy cooks, they require little preparation. Just remove the ends and any strings, wash, drain, and cook quickly. Steam for about 10 minutes in a little boiling water, toss with butter, and serve. Or stir-fry for 2 to 3 minutes in sesame oil and toss with a bit of soy sauce.

Ideally they should be cooked as soon as they're picked. If it's more convenient, pick them early in the morning, rinse in cold water, drain, and refrigerate in the vegetable compartment. They'll be all ready to stem and cook for dinner, and the flavor will still be first rate. I've kept them as long as a week in the refrigerator. To keep them longer than that, blanch them, drain thoroughly, and freeze for out-of-season use.

Asparagus Pea

Si Jiao Dou, Sz Kok Dau

Psophocarpus tetragonolobus

(color photo, page xiii)

This is an easy vegetable to grow and a lot of fun to serve to unsuspecting guests. The whole plant is edible, including the leaves, shoots, flowers, and even roots, though people usually grow it for its pods. The protein-rich pods grow in great profusion and taste just like asparagus.

The asparagus pea is a legume, as you might expect from its name. It's also called goa bean, winged bean (from its shape), and four-angled bean. (Do not confuse it with the asparagus bean, which is another name for the Chinese yard-long bean.) It originated in India and soon spread throughout Asia as far as New Guinea. Today it is an important crop from China to Africa to the West Indies, in part because of its high protein content.

Appearance

The asparagus pea is a rampant vine and can take over any area in which you plant them, so grow them in an out-of-the-way corner. The pale blue flowers, which whiten with age, are very showy and attractive, so you can grow it as an ornamental edible. It competes successfully with most weeds.

The pods are very oddly shaped; they grow sort of square instead of rounded and have four sides. If left to mature, they eventually reach about 8 inches long. Each side has a prominent winged edge that makes it an attractive and unusual vegetable to serve, especially if you slice it crosswise. They look unusual, even before you savor the asparagus flavor.

How to Grow

With a growth habit similar to that of pole beans, asparagus pea vines grow to 10 feet long and require staking.

Getting started. The asparagus pea is not frost-tender and can be sown in the garden a couple of weeks before the last frost date in your area. It does best in cool weather. Since it has a long harvesting season, the earlier you start it the better. With vegetables of this sort I usually gamble a bit; if I'm unlucky and have a hard frost after I've sown my seeds, all I'm out is a little seed and a few minutes' work. Most of the time I find my gamble pays off.

Planting. Plant seeds ½ inch deep and about 6 inches apart, in rows 18 inches apart. By the time you finish harvesting, it will be July just in time to put in a fall crop of something else.

Growing needs. Asparagus pea isn't fussy about soil and does well in any halfway decent garden soil. Fertilize when flowers appear and at three-week intervals after that. Either side-dress with a balanced fertilizer or water with a fish-and-seaweed fertilizer. This is a carefree vegetable: sow it and forget it. What more could you want?

How to Harvest

About 50 days after sowing, begin harvesting the pods. If you wish to eat the leaves, shoots, or flowers, gather these earlier when they're tender.

Sample the roots in about 35 days, then try them again in 50 days. The longer you let them grow, the greater the crop you'll get, but you may prefer the flavor of the younger roots.

Varieties

Two different vegetables go by the name asparagus pea. The other one is a different species (*Lotus tetragonolobus*) and much smaller. To confuse things even more, the alternate name of *L. tetragonolobus* is winged pea. Plants grow only 12 to 18 inches tall, and the pods reach only about 3 inches long at maturity. The showy flowers are red to maroon, not pale blue. Again, you can eat the shoots and roots as well as the pods. For best eating, gather pods of this species when they're only an inch long.

The asparagus flavor of the asparagus pea pods is most noticeable when they're gathered well before they are fully mature, ideally, when not more than an inch long.

ASPARAGUS PEA PODS may be prepared in a variety of ways:

- Stir-fry, alone or in combination with meat or other vegetables.
- Sliver and cook briefly in a clear broth, and garnish with shredded scallions.
- Add to stews when the cooking is almost complete.
- Serve by themselves, boiled briefly and tossed with oil and a very little seasoning.
- Cold pods, cooked crisp-tender, are delicious in salad.

SHOOTS, LEAVES, AND FLOWERS. In addition to the pods, the whole plant is edible. The tender new shoots, young leaves, and pretty blue flowers are delicately delicious. They make a fine addition to curries and clear soups. The flowers make an especially attractive garnish for a salad, and the leaves can be cooked like spinach.

ROOTS. The roots are also edible. Since asparagus peas grow so abundantly, you may feel you can sacrifice some of the plants to sample the roots. Dig when young (try after 35 days) and cook in any way you'd cook a sweet potato. Added to Indian dahl they are superb. Thinly sliced, they make an interesting and authentic addition to stir-fried beef and snow peas. You may find yourself growing this fascinating vegetable for the roots alone, as they do in Myanmar (formerly Burma).

SHELLED AND ROASTED. Since the plant bears so abundantly, it's entirely possible that you won't be able to keep up with harvesting the pods. If the peas get past the green eating stage, all is not lost. Just let pods grow to their full 8 inches in length before you pick them, then shell and roast the peas in the oven. Combine with hot brown rice for an interesting accompaniment to chop suey or sukiyaki. Or salt them lightly and serve as a snack or with drinks instead of roasted soybeans or peanuts.

Chinese Radish

Loh Bo, Loh Baak

Raphanus sativus

(color photo, page xiii)

In our cuisine, nothing is simpler than the radish. We serve it up in a relish dish or slice some into a tossed salad. In China, the uses of this simple vegetable are incredibly numerous: radishes are grated, steamed, stir-fried, pickled, boiled, sculptured for great banquet dishes, and dried. Chinese radish may also be called daikon or Oriental radish.

Many gardeners don't appreciate the versatility of radishes. You can eat them at various stages of maturity, starting with the thinnings. Even the leaves can be eaten before the roots form or when the roots are barely showing their shape. If you tire of them, you can even let plants go to seed and eat the pods and the seeds.

Appearance

There is great variety among Asian radishes, from round, to long and tapered, to short and blunt-ended, and with colors ranging from pure white to rose pink, purple, and black. The biggeset difference from radishes found in North America is the enormous sizes of some Asian varieties. They are all deliciously edible and, in season, are an everyday feature of an Asian meal. Some varieties have decorative foiliage.

How to Grow

Getting started. Check each variety to determine whether to sow in spring, summer, or fall. Aside from planting dates, all radishes are cultivated the same way and are the easiest of all vegetables to grow. They germinate practically overnight.

The larger varieties need loose, loamy soil, so dig down 2 feet when preparing the planting area, as you do for carrots. Incorporate compost and balanced fertilizer before planting.

Planting. Sow seeds ½ inch deep and 2 inches apart. How much you thin depends on what variety you planted; obviously a radish that reaches 5 inches in diameter needs more space than small varieties. Thin in stages and eat the thinnings.

Growing needs. Like any root vegetable, Asian radishes need ample and deep watering, and they benefit from mulch to keep down weeds. The long-season fall and winter radishes need supplemental feeding. Side-dress with a balanced fertilizer (ideally one lower in nitrogen, such as 4-6-6) or water with a fish-and-seaweed product every three to four weeks.

Pest potential. If root maggots have been a problem, grow under row covers. Mounding wood ashes or powdered cayenne pepper around seedlings may discourage these pests, but row covers offers the best protection.

DID YOU KNOW?

The cultivation of radishes is ancient. The Egyptians have known and used them for over 5,000 years, the Chinese perhaps even longer. Although we don't think of radishes as containing much nourishment, they were part of the diet the pharaohs fed the builders of the great pyramids — along with garlic and onions — to get more work out of them. The Chinese consider radishes marvelously healthful, and throughout the centuries radishes have had a reputation for stimulating the appetite. Some old herbals recommended it as a cure for melancholy, and I can see how the crisp, pleasantly pungent nibble of a chilled radish might have a cheering effect.

How to Harvest

Since you can eat the leaves, roots, pods, and seeds, the time of harvest depends entirely on your appetite and patience. Late-season radishes even hold in the ground for some time after reaching maturity. They also store well in the refrigerator or in moist sand in a cool, but not freezing, environment. They keep indefinitely if pickled or dried.

Varieties

Choosing among radish varieties is like confronting a tray of French pastries: they all look good. Fortunately, you can have your pastry and eat it too because most radishes take up so little room and grow so quickly that in a single season you can try out several different kinds.

Chinese radishes aren't always identified as such but may be called "fall and winter" radishes. Some catalogs use "daikon" for all Asian radishes, although this is just a specific variety. Others differentiate between Chinese and Japanese varieties when they may be popular in both countries. Once you get into radishes, you'll learn to recognize different kinds regardless of catalog descriptions.

Be careful about "icicle" radishes. This name is given to both a white traditional variety and a white Asian variety, and they are not at all alike. Chances are if it's offered for spring sowing, it is the ordinary one; for fall sowing, the Asian one.

There are spring, summer, and fall Asian radishes, but the bulk of them are for fall sowing. Many can be stored over the winter as easily as carrots or turnips. Choose your variety according to when you want to harvest your crop.

Varieties to look for: Ta-Mei-Hwa, Tsin-tao Green, Nam Pan.

Once you get accustomed to using radishes as an all-around vegetable, you'll be amazed at all the years you neglected them.

RAW, GRATED. In China and Japan, radishes are a favorite ingredient in the little dishes of dipping sauce served with tempura and other cooked meat-and-vegetable dishes. You can also:

- Shred or finely grate the radishes, then mix with soy sauce.

- Place the grated radish on one side along with a little pile of grated ginger, and the diner chooses one or both to add to the soy sauce.

- Grated radish blended with a little Asian sesame oil is a simple but surprisingly effective combination. This makes an excellent garnish or antipasto.

- Use grated radish instead of onion on your next hamburger or on a corned-beef sandwich.

- Grated radish instead of sauerkraut on a hot dog is a whole new ball game.

COOKED. Another new world opens up the minute you realize that radishes are good cooked:

- Stir-fry with cucumber and chives and a little garlic in Asian sesame oil; add a little chicken broth, cover, and simmer 5 minutes. All the vegetables should be cut into pieces of the same size so they cook at the same rate.

- The Chinese like icicle radish stir-fried with shellfish such as shrimp. Peel and shred the radish. Stir-fry scallions first, then the radish, then the shrimp. The entire cooking time shouldn't be over 6 or 8 minutes. Add a little soy sauce just before serving and perhaps a tiny bit of sake (rice wine) or sherry.

- Stir-fry works very well with some diced pineapple and pork instead of shrimp.

- Grated radishes are also added to many Chinese sauces.

PICKLED. Asian radishes are widely used as pickles. Some recipes, like regular pickles, take a long time to cure. But others can be made in a few hours simply by slicing the radishes very thin and marinating in sugar, water, and rice vinegar. An entirely different taste is achieved by marinating in rice wine and soy sauce with a little sugar. Pickled radishes are often used in cooking, where they impart their spicy flavor to the whole dish in a very subtle way.

FOLIAGE. Perhaps you never knew that the foliage of radishes is edible. Young radish tops make excellent greens, briefly steamed and served simply with a little butter.

SEEDS. Radish seeds are pleasantly peppery and great in a tossed salad.

Chinese Eggplant

GIE ZI, NGAI KWA
Solanum melongena
(color photo, page xiii)

The eggplant is a native of tropical Asia and is very popular in China. The cuisines of the Middle East, Russia, and India also use eggplant in many interesting dishes, so eggplant can take you on a culinary trip around the world. Also know as aubergine, eggplant was long grown in Europe and England purely as an ornamental, which tells you how pretty it is.

Appearance

Aubergine is a lovely plant in flower, even prettier when loaded with fruit. The compact plants grow 1½ to 2 feet and are interestingly shaped. Eggplant flowers are lavender, but the Asian varieties tend to have flowers of a much deeper hue. According to variety, eggplants are various shades of purple, brown, green, cream, snow white, gray, or striped. The shapes vary from almost round to narrow and elongated like a zucchini. They are beautifully glossy and very decorative.

How to Grow

Getting started. Eggplants are long-season, warm-weather vegetables. Although you can successfully sow seeds directly in the ground if your growing season is long enough, you may want to start seeds indoors.

Planting. Eggplant seeds are slow to germinate. To speed things up, soak the seeds overnight and plant immediately the next morning, about a month before outdoor planting time. Sow seeds ¼ to ½ inch deep.

Transplanting outdoors. Eggplants shouldn't be set outside until warm weather has settled in, usually about two weeks after your last frost date. Figure back for your area and start seeds indoors about eight weeks before planting out. (See page 201.)

Before setting out your transplants, harden them off for two weeks. Set plants 2 feet apart in rows 3 feet apart. Some dwarf varieties can go closer. When preparing the bed for the transplants, cultivate deeply and dig a hole 8 inches deep. Put a cup of balanced fertilizer and 2 cups of compost in the bottom of the hole. Mix the soil you're going to use to fill the hole with a cup of this same mixture. Set in your seedlings at the same height they were growing in their containers, and water thoroughly once you've firmed down the earth around the plant. Keep moist the first 10 days but do not soak them.

Growing needs. Eggplant is a heavy feeder and requires regular, deep watering. During the growing season, fertilize every four weeks. Compost is a good choice, especially if mixed with a little balanced fertilizer. Avoid giving plants too much nitrogen, or plants may produce more leaves than fruits. Water as needed to keep soil evenly moist for the best-tasting eggplants. Mulch about 2 inches deep to help keep soil moist.

How to Harvest

Mature Asian eggplants are smaller than the ones you're probably used to. The size at maturity depends on which variety you're growing; ranging from the size of a large egg to a medium zucchini. Pick eggplants immature rather than fully ripened, before seeds are brown. The skin should be glossy and smooth; dull skin is a sign of being over ripe.

Pick eggplants often and the plants will bear for months — a four-month fruiting period is not unusual where the growing season is long enough. If you're used to classic large Italian varieties such as 'Black Beauty', you'll be stunned the first time you grow an Asian variety. Instead of a crop of 8 or 10 you may find yourself picking 30 or 40 from a single plant.

Varieties

Good varieties abound, most of them much earlier than standard eggplants.

Varieties to look for: Ping Tung, Hybrid Purple Excel, Ma-Zu Purple.

Asian eggplants aren't bitter and don't need peeling or pre-salting before cooking.

FRIED OR ROASTED EGGPLANT. In China, it's stir-fried with bean sprouts, peppers, and tomatoes. In Japan, it's cooked tempura-style. In Italy, it's floured and sautéed in olive oil. In Russia and the Middle East, it's combined with olive oil, chopped onion, and chopped tomato, plus salt and pepper, and served as a cold relish.

"THE SULTAN FAINTED." This famous dish is made by stuffing large eggplants with roasted eggplant combined with pine nuts, ground lamb, tomatoes, coriander, garlic, and lemon juice.

PICKLES. Pickling styles differ in different parts of the world.

- Greek. Submerge sliced eggplants in hot vinegar that has been simmered with lemon juice, garlic, and water, allow to cool, and refrigerate for a month or two.

- Italian. Use garlic and olive oil in the pickling fluid.

- American. Use any standard pickling recipe. Even simpler, try simmering them for 5 minutes in the pickle liquid left over from a jar of commercial pickles. Cool and refrigerate; eat in about a week. The smaller varieties work best for pickles.

AN INDIAN CLASSIC. Bake eggplants at 350°F until soft (about 30 to 60 minutes). Scoop out pulp and season with garam masala, or an Indian spice mix of ginger, cloves, turmeric, coriander, and a green chili pepper, minced. (Adjust heat by adjusting the number of chilis.) Add 2 chopped tomatoes, a couple of thinly sliced carrots, 1 or 2 potatoes, 1 onion, and 3 cups peas. Sauté all in safflower oil for about 15 minutes. This can be made the day before; refrigerate and reheat later. Serve as is or stuff filling back into eggplant halves and sprinkle with breadcrumbs and minced parsley.

OTHER USES. Eggplant makes great kabobs with tomatoes, peppers, and small white cooked onions threaded alternately along the skewer, with or without meat. Cut into chunks and marinate in your favorite marinade recipe.

6

THE CHINESE HERB GARDEN

BUNCHING ONION • GARLIC • GARLIC CHIVES •
HOT PEPPER • CILANTRO • MITSUBA
• WATERCRESS • SESAME • GINGER

Many herbs in this chapter are familiar, some unfamiliar. All of them are good eating and contribute to the delightfully different flavors that characterize Asian cooking. If you want your Chinese dishes to be authentic, or even if you merely want to bring some interesting new changes to favorite old recipes, learn to grow and use this sampling of Chinese herbs. As a bonus, you'll find that many are beautiful and can be combined with flowers for a striking and unusual display.

In China, herbs are valued for more than just flavor. Many herbs are accepted in Chinese medicine as beneficial; some have been used for thousands of years. There are famous herb gardens in China and Japan that contain plants from all over Asia, as well as from Europe and Africa. In earlier times, such gardens were so cherished that special herbs grown in them were among the presents offered in tribute to the reigning emperor. Some were sponsored and supported by the rulers of these countries, though private herb gardens were also cultivated. Herbal medicine has been the subject of scholarly study for centuries in China, and this research continues today.

Bunching Onion

Cong, Chin Choong

Allium fistulosum

(color photo, page xv)

Bunching onions are known by many names. You may find them in seed catalogs as Japanese leek, nebuka, scallion, spring onion, multiplier onion, green onion, and Welsh onion. Bunching onions are native to Siberia and have no botanical connection with Wales, though they do look a little like leeks and are a common crop in Welsh gardens.

They're more economical than immature onions, since they increase in number throughout a long season, while an onion produces a single immature scallion at the expense of a mature bulb. So, grow your regular onions to maturity and plant these true scallions for your green onions.

Bunching onions are an excellent vegetable: easy, prolific, mild or pungent depending on the season, and well worth the small space they take in the garden. They are unusually hardy and can sometimes be harvested when it means brushing aside the snow to get at them. I never have enough scallions, so these are a joy. I don't have to choose between my onion crop and early scallions, or feel guilty at the thought that I'm sacrificing a large onion.

Appearance

Bunching onions are scallions, and that's what they look like. They differ in one important respect from ordinary young onion shoots: The clumps grow with several "scallions" bunched together, as if you planted too many seeds in one spot. It is easy to see why they are called bunching onions. The shoots divide into more shoots as they grow, and they are harvested by pulling shoots away from the main bunch when you want some to eat. Each shoot is a whole scallion.

The stalks are silvery white and about ¾ inch in diameter. Usually they grow 12 to 14 inches tall, but some varieties may be shorter or taller. Plants grow into compact clumps that are easy to tuck into various corners of the garden.

How to Grow

Getting started. Plant seeds early in spring for summer use, or in July or August for fall or very early spring use. They are winter hardy almost everywhere; mulch in areas where the winters are severe. If you're growing them on your windowsill, sow them anytime.

Planting. Sow small seeds about ½ inch deep and 2 inches apart. Don't sow in boring rows like ordinary vegetables but in clumps throughout the garden as an accent plant.

Growing needs. Give bunching onions a moderately rich soil with good drainage if you want spectacular plants. Dig in compost and a balanced fertilizer before planting, and feed once a month with liquid fertilizer or a fish-and-seaweed product. Water normally, but don't overdo it.

They require little care other than weeding and multiply readily. If you let plants flower, they'll self-sow. You only have to plant once for a lifetime supply. Divide two- to three-year-old clumps in spring or early summer to prevent overcrowding and increase your supply.

How to Harvest

This species matures in about 65 days. To gather, use one hand to pull an onion gently away from the others, using the other hand to hold the clump so it's not uprooted. The remaining onions will go on growing. If you don't need the whole

DID YOU KNOW?

For many American gardeners, scallions are as much a sign of spring as the first robin, but as often as not, these are merely immature onions. True scallions never form a bulb; they are perennial plants that will continue to grow in clumps but never turn into an onion no matter how long they grow.

onion, harvest just a few of the leaves as if they were chives. (I find it easier to grow chives for that purpose.)

Varieties

Several types of "bulbless" or bunching-type onions (scallions) are available. It is sometimes sold as the variety 'Evergreen Hardy White' because it's the most winter hardy of all the bunching-type onions.

Multiplier onions (*Allium cepa* Proliferum Group) are another type of perennial onion. These are some-times confused with bunching onions, but they differ in that they form tiny clusters of bulblets at the tops of their stems. If you remove and plant these bulblets, you'll get nice green onions early the following spring. If you don't remove them, they'll plant themselves, which is how they got their other name, walking onion. These are also known by the names topsetting onion and Egyptian onion.

Varieties to look for: Evergreen, Red Beard, Four Season.

— CULINARY USES —

Since bunching onions are scallions, use them any way you use scallions. In Asian cuisine they're cut into little brushes as a garnish, sliced thinly for clear soups, or sautéed briefly at the start of a stir-fry dish. Early in the year they're mild enough to enjoy raw. As the season progresses and the stems thicken, the flavor becomes a little too pungent for most people to eat out of hand. This is when they come into their own in cooked dishes.

COOKED SCALLIONS. If you've never prepared them as a braised vegetable, you'll find this delicate and unusual enough to serve as a company dish. It takes only minutes to prepare. Cut the whole onion in half vertically, from green stalk right down through the white part. Sauté in a little sesame oil until golden brown, add enough chicken broth to simmer, cover, and cook for 5 minutes. If you want, stir in a little soy sauce just before serving, but I like the golden look of the vegetable without the soy. The flavor is as different from the fresh onion as braised leeks are from raw leeks, more delicious than you can imagine.

Garlic
Suan, Suen Tou
Allium sativum
(color photo, page xiv)

The use of garlic goes far back beyond recorded history. In Chinese writing, it's designated by a single symbol, proof that a word is very old. A native of western Asia, garlic was introduced to China in prehistoric time. The Chinese consider garlic a medicine as well as an essential ingredient in their cuisine. It's sold in health-food stores throughout the United States in the form of tablets, but why not enjoy it in cooking instead?

Appearance
The leaves of garlic are narrow but flat and solid (not hollow like chives). Plants grow to about 18 inches tall. A flower stem rises up along with the leaves, and the pinkish lavender flower cluster opens from a papery sheath that never fully parts as with other alliums.

How to Grow
Getting started. Plant garlic cloves in place outdoors in late fall (about the time of your first frost date, or even later). You can plant garlic in early spring, but you'll get smaller cloves. The larger the clove you plant, the better the crop.

Planting. Separate garlic bulbs into individual cloves, and plant them ½ inches deep, about 6 inches apart and in rows at least a foot apart. (Space elephant garlic cloves 7 to 8 inches apart.) If you're not planning to mulch and your winters are cold, plant 2 inches deep. Incorporate a balanced fertilizer before planting.

Growing needs. Garlic likes a sunny location and a fertile, sandy loam. Plants grow most briskly when the temperature is over 65°F and the days are long. It's very undemanding and can mostly be left to itself. Fertilize once a month and be careful not to overwater. If flower stems (known as *scapes*) form at the top of your plants, snip these off to allow the plant to put all its energy into bulb formation. These flower scapes make good eating.

How to Harvest

Cloves mature in six to eight months. You don't have to guess when the bulb is ready to harvest; the tops will turn brown and dry. If they turn brown but not dry, bend them down and they'll dry quickly. Sometimes, when you dig up a clump, the bulb is immature because of vagaries in the weather, soil conditions, and so forth. Replant it; it will give you a mature bulb next season.

Leave bulbs in the sun for a day or two to dry (take in at night if you don't have a sunny porch). Shorten the tops and cut roots off close to the base of the bulb. Leave the bulb whole; don't divide it into cloves until you need one.

Store in open baskets or other containers as you do onions; air circulation is important. Once in a while, turn bulbs and check to see if any have molded; sometimes only part of a bulb is spoiled and the rest can be set aside to use in the near future.

Varieties

A related species, known as elephant garlic (da tou suan, dai suen tou, *Allium ampeloprasum*), is of particular interest. Though more closely related to leeks, it looks like a bigger version of ordinary garlic. Under ideal conditions a single bulb can weigh over a pound (usually more like a half pound), and a clump can grow as wide as a dinner plate. If this sounds unwieldy for the small garden, it isn't really. This kind of garlic is much more prolific than common garlic, so you need fewer plants. This species is hardy to about 20°F, so a straw mulch is advisable over the winter in severe climates. This enormous variety is as mild as it is big. The oversized cloves peel in a jiffy — especially if you first crush them with the flat side of a wide-bladed knife. The garlic flavor is pleasant but not overpowering, especially useful in salads where ordinary raw garlic might offend an unwary diner.

— CULINARY USES —

All of the uses described here apply to elephant garlic as well as common garlic, but elephant garlic has a milder flavor. For cooking, peel whole garlic cloves before use. You may prefer to crush slightly and remove from the dish before serving. If cooked slightly in a little oil, the flavor will be distributed throughout the dish.

The curling scapes that form at the top of garlic can be used like common chives or garlic chives. They are milder than garlic cloves and add a pretty bit of green as a garnish on omelettes, creamed vegetables, and clear soups.

Suggestions for using the cloves, include the following:

- Blend in butter as a spread for making garlic bread.

- Mix with cottage or cream cheese, adding parsley or grated carrot for color and additional flavor.

- Make a garlic vinegar to use in your salad dressings: simply peel a garlic clove and drop it in a small container of vinegar; after three or four days, it will impart a garlic flavor and can then be removed.

- Rub leg of lamb with fresh rosemary and insert slivers of garlic in slits throughout the surface.

Garlic Chives

Jiu Cai, Gow Choy

Allium tuberosum

(color photo, page xiv)

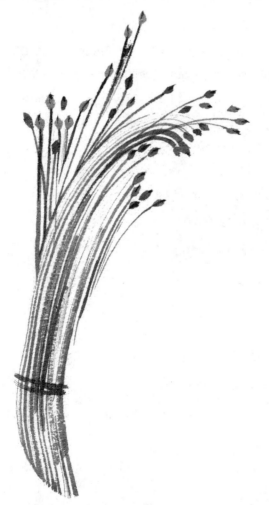

Most gardeners grow common chives, for both their culinary uses and their attractive lavender blooms, which make a pretty display over a long time. Garlic chives are closely related to common chives, but they're as different as they can be. The flavor is garlic instead of onion, the flowers white instead of lavender.

The individual bulbs are large enough to be useful and give rise to another alternate name, Chinese leek. This herb is also popular in Japan, where it is known as *nira*. Garlic chives, sometimes called Chinese chives, can't be purchased in the average supermarket. You must grow them if you want to have them, and nothing could be easier. They're a very useful and beautiful herb — indoors and out — and you'll become very fond of them.

Because garlic chives tolerate less-than-ideal soil and moisture conditions, they make excellent plants for the rock garden, nestling into out-of-the-way corners and sending up their lovely blooms right on schedule every year. They're among the most ornamental choices for an herb garden. The flowers are so attractive you can tuck them into flower beds; the plants are more compact and less sprawly than common chives.

Appearance

Garlic or Chinese chives can always be recognized by their broad flat leaves, unlike the smaller rounded stems of common chives. The star-shaped flowers are usually white and arrayed in a dome rather than a sphere. Some flowers are lavender but larger than those of common chives.

How to Grow

Getting started. Indoors, garlic chives can be planted anytime you please. Or buy a plant from an herb nursery. Once you have a clump going, you'll have a permanent supply and will soon be handing pots around to happy neighbors. Chives are unfussy and prolific, and that combination is hard to beat.

Planting. Garlic chives germinate just as slowly as common chives, so if you start from seeds, patiently keep the soil moist until the tiny shoots are well on their way. You can start seeds indoors or out; sow about ½ inch deep. Once the seedlings are about two weeks old, let the soil dry out somewhat between waterings; from then on treat them as you do common chives.

Growing needs. Garlic chives transplant easily and settle quickly into a new location. For large plantings, set month-old transplants 12 to 14 inches apart in rows about 20 inches apart.

Garlic chives aren't fussy and thrive in almost any soil, rich or coarse and gravelly. They prefer full sun but tolerate partial shade. Fertilize lightly after harvest; otherwise, an annual side-dressing of compost will keep them growing well.

You can dig up and divide clumps that have grown too large for their site in either spring or fall. Separate and pot up a clump in early fall and grow it in your kitchen all winter. The plants you leave outdoors will die back during the winter and come up again in the spring.

DID YOU KNOW?

If you have trouble with chipmunks invading your tulip beds, a generous planting of garlic chives sometimes discourages them and other rodents. I can only suppose that they don't like the taste and consequently leave the tulip bulbs alone. This is not a guaranteed solution, but it's easier and a lot more decorative than planting tulips in wire cages.

How to Harvest

Harvest leaves any time after they're about 6 inches high. Cut each shoot to within 2 inches of the ground and take several shoots all the way to that point. Don't clip across the entire plant; the bulbs need some foliage to grow on.

If you want flowers, leave some clumps unclipped until the flower stalks have developed. You can clip a little and still get flowers, but let them flower the first time around until you become familiar with the growth habit of this herb.

Once you have enough to spare, treat yourself to the buds and flowers; these are delicious raw or added to cooked dishes at the very last minute. They can be harvested whenever they appear, at any stage.

Don't let the flowers go to seed; it takes energy away from the plant, and spent flowers aren't particularly attractive. Cut them all off to eat fresh or to dry. Once your garlic chives are well established you'll always have enough to enjoy the beautiful blossoms and for the kitchen as well.

Varieties

Plants in the trade are often confused, or at least their names are, so you may get a different species when you go looking for garlic chives. At least one has lavender flowers rather than white; this variant is garlic-scented but not strongly so. Another is *Allium victorialis*, also known as alpine leek. All that have a garlic flavor are grown and used in China.

The most desirable, in my opinion, is the fragrant species. It sometimes goes by the name Chinese chives but is also called fragrant-flowered garlic, and it's frequently confused with garlic chives. Now classified as *Allium ramosum*, it was formerly called *A. odoratum* because its flowers are quite fragrant — they smell like roses! Two or three pots on a windowsill can perfume your kitchen and are as pretty as any flowering house plant.

Garlic chives can be used exactly as you use common chives, if you allow for the stronger garlic flavor:

- Mix with cottage cheese or yogurt.
- Mince for salads.
- Sprinkle as a garnish over stuffed eggs.
- Toss with bean sprouts for a quick high-protein salad.

IN COOKED DISHES. Garlic chives are a zesty addition to cooked dishes as well. Add during the last few minutes of cooking, as they tend to get stringy when overcooked, and lose much of their flavor. The Chinese often add garlic chives to recipes calling for onions and garlic. They feel the chives enhance the flavor of these other alliums.

GARLIC CHIVE BULBS. The bulbs too can be eaten, like garlic or shallots. The flavor is much more delicate than garlic, yet different from the mild shallot; experiment with them boldly. Don't eat your entire crop; leave some bulbs for next year's crop or your winter indoor garden. Here are some ideas:

- Crush and add to boiling vinegar, then set aside for a few days to mellow.
- Mince and braise with meat or sprinkle over fish before broiling.
- Heat in melted butter before scrambling eggs.

CHIVE BLOSSOMS. All chive blossoms are edible and can be eaten fresh or dried. I always keep a couple of dried bunches handy and find many unexpected uses for them. They're much milder than either the leaves or the bulbs and make a very pretty garnish.

- Separate into florets to float on top of a clear soup; add after the individual bowls have been filled so that they come to the table fresh and still faintly fragrant.
- Give vichyssoise an exotic touch by adding chive blossoms along with the traditional chives.

Hot Pepper

La Jiao, Lat Jiao

Capsicum frutescens

(color photo, page xv)

Although I would classify sweet peppers as a vegetable rather than as an herb, hot peppers or chilis are never eaten as a vegetable — not even in China, where they are an essential ingredient in Hunan and Szechwan cookery. I have therefore put hot peppers where the Chinese would plant them: in the herb garden.

Pepper is so much a part of Asian cuisine that it is necessary to differentiate these hot peppers from other types of pepper you may encounter in the spice section of Chinese grocery. Szechwan peppercorns, for example, are the dried berries from the prickly ash tree (*Zanthoxylum ailanthoides*).

Chinese hot peppers are native American chili peppers that Asian countries have taken as their own. They are not used in classic Cantonese or Mandarin cooking but are an authentic ingredient in dishes originating in many of the other Chinese cuisines. They were discovered by Columbus in his search for a route to the Spice Islands of the East; he brought them back to Europe, where they were warmly received. The Portuguese took them to India and Asia, where their use and culture spread so widely that for some time botanists thought those lands were their native habitat.

Hot peppers are very easy to grow and take up little space in the garden. The plants are decorative and fit perfectly at home in the flower bed.

Appearance

Peppers are so beautiful and graceful a plant that they used to be grown as ornamentals. Even today florists offer an "ornamental pepper," which is a popular houseplant. Since hot pepper plants are just as pretty as ornamental peppers, and edible too, why not grow them instead?

Peppers flower freely, with numerous white to greenish white blossoms that are very decorative against the glossy, dark green leaves. A pepper plant, like an orange tree (and many other vegetable plants), bears its flowers and fruits simultaneously; a bush full of pretty white flowers and peppers in various colors from green to yellow to red, hanging straight down in colorful profusion, is worthy of your patio or terrace.

How to Grow

Getting started. Peppers are strictly a warm-weather plant and do not tolerate the slightest frost. Start seeds indoors about eight weeks before transplanting outside, and wait to plant until the soil is warm.

Planting. Sow seeds ½ inch deep and 4 seeds per inch in a shallow flat. The seeds may be slow to germinate, and you can speed up this step by placing them in a warm spot or using a heat mat. Transplant the seedlings as soon as the first pair of true leaves appears; space them 2 to 3 inches apart, or plant in individual cell-type containers.

Transplanting outdoors. As soon as the seedlings are reasonably large and sturdy, harden off to prepare them for transplanting outside. In the ground, space them 18 to 24 inches apart in rows 24 to 36 inches apart. Before putting the plants in place, dig a hole for each one 6 inches deeper than the plants will be set. Fill with compost plus a half cup of balanced fertilizer. Then fill the hole with regular garden soil.

DID YOU KNOW?

Nutritionists have long known that chilis are rich sources of vitamins A, C, and B_6. They are also high in niacin, riboflavin, and thiamin as well as minerals including iron, magnesium, phosphorus, and potassium. All in all, if you enjoy chilis, eat them with a clear conscience; they not only taste wonderful, they're good for you.

Growing needs. Keep well watered. Fertilize when the blossoms first appear and when peppers are about an inch long. They respond well to compost and a side-dressing of 5-10-10. You may find you need to add extra nitrogen occasionally, but if you overfertilize, especially with too much nitrogen, you'll get beautiful foliage but little fruit.

How to Harvest

You can pick hot peppers at almost any stage of their growth. Their color indicates their age; for most varieties yellow or green is early, orange is getting mature, red is mature. For drying, allow peppers to reach maturity. Once they reach maturity, pick them and the plants will continue to bear fruit for months.

CAUTION!

Don't rub your eyes before washing your hands when you have handled hot peppers; the capsicum, a volatile oil that makes them "hot," can irritate tender tissue. Cutting hot peppers may irritate skin; if your skin is sensitive, wear rubber gloves.

Varieties

Most hot peppers turn red, though some, like 'Hungarian Wax', start out bright yellow rather than green. You can make your own hot pepper sauce with the tabasco pepper (*Capsicum frutescens* var. *tabasco*); the jalapeño, one of the hottest, will bring tears to your eyes. All hot varieties are delicious and only experience will enable you to differentiate among them. You can grow peppers that are hot or hotter, so try several varieties and then settle down to the ones that suit you best.

You'll find at least one variety listed in almost every catalog, except the ones that offer only Asian seeds. Look through several to get a wider selection. The smaller varieties are the ones grown in China and are the most decorative to dry.

Varieties to look for: Chi-Chien, Hybrid Golden Hot, Goat Horn.

While hot peppers must be used with discretion, they enhance a wide variety of cuisines. They can be used both fresh and dried. Strings of dried red or green chilis hung from the kitchen ceiling are a colorful as well as practical winter decoration.

STIR-FRY. To make a typical hot stir-fry dish, start with 1 chili pepper. (If that's not hot enough, try 2 the next time you make it.) Stir-fry thinly sliced beef in peanut oil for 5 minutes, then add sliced scallions, minced ginger, and sliced chili pepper, plus a little soy sauce and a small amount of water. Stir-fry another minute and add snow peas. Stir-fry for 1 more minute, thicken the sauce with a little cornstarch, and serve with white rice.

WITH EGGPLANT. A tasty and spicy eggplant dish starts with roasted eggplant. Take the hot roasted eggplant out of its skin and combine with cut-up fresh tomatoes, green beans, 1 or 2 onions, peas, a couple of minced chilis, and 3 raw potatoes, cut up. Cook all together in a covered skillet with a little olive oil until the tomatoes are soft but not mushy. Salt to taste and serve hot or cold.

SAUCE FOR FISH. Chili peppers and scallions, thinly sliced and fried lightly in oil, make a delicious sauce for broiled fish. If the flavor is too strong for you, discard the peppers and scallions after frying and use just the oil to dress the fish.

WITH PICKLES. If you make pickles, add a fresh chili pepper to the jar when you put it away to "ripen"; remove the chili when serving the pickles.

DID YOU KNOW?

Hot peppers and garlic whirled in a blender with plain water make a spray that deters many insects when misted on the foliage of your plants; it may even discourage an occasional woodchuck.

Cilantro

XIAN CHOY, YAN SUI

Coriandrum sativum

(color photo, page xiv)

Many people are surprised to learn that coriander seeds and the leafy herb cilantro are from the same plant. Anyone who's grown it — who's seen the delicate white flowers mature into the familiar round seeds, which scatter over the garden to plant next year's crop — knows better. Some people refer to all parts of the plant as coriander, and that's how it used to be listed in the herb section of seed catalogs.

Now that the greens are so popular in recipes from many different countries, suppliers tend to list it under cilantro. In Asian markets, when looking for fresh bunches of this herb, ask for Chinese parsley (or use the Chinese name); in Latin American markets, or when traveling in Mexico or Italy, ask for cilantro. Cookbooks usually distinguish between the fresh green leaves and the seeds by using the term "coriander" for the seeds only.

Coriander was used in Egyptian cookery 3,000 years ago; natives of Mexico and South America have long eaten it extensively. It is absolutely essential if you wish to prepare authentic Chinese dishes. Chinese cookbooks describe it as aromatic and delicately scented.

At the market, a bunch of cilantro looks a lot like a bunch of flat-leaved Italian parsley. The flavor is unique, however, and bears no resemblance to Italian parsley. You can also distinguish the two by their smell, as cilantro has a much stronger smell than parsley when you rub a leaf.

Like most herbs, coriander has an ancient history, with a rich vein of mythology. It was used in love potions and as a general aphrodisiac. It is one of the herbs mentioned in the Bible, in Exodus and in Numbers, where manna is described as "white like coriander seed."

Appearance

Cilantro is a pretty plant with lacy, flat sprays of white to palest lavender flowers. It grows about 2 feet tall and has leaves of two different shapes. The bottom leaves look something like Italian parsley; the top leaves are much more deeply cut and feathery.

DID YOU KNOW?

Coriander flowers attract beneficial insects. Though cutting flower buds prolongs your harvest of the leaves, plant enough so you can let some plants bloom and go to seed. You'll enjoy the pretty flowers, and you'll attract pollinators and other beneficial insects to your garden.

How to Grow

Getting started. You can plant cilantro any time from early spring through late summer. It takes about 50 days to produce a good crop of leaves and 90 to 105 days to produce seeds, so you don't need to start seeds indoors. Transplanted seedlings usually bolt earlier than plants sown in place, so there's no particular advantage to starting seeds indoors.

Coriander grows best in full sun, though it will take a little shade. In hot climates, it actually grows better with a little shade. Ordinary garden soil is fine. You can also enjoy cilantro year-round by growing it indoors. It does very well in a container on a sunny windowsill.

Planting. Barely cover the seeds with soil and sow ½ inch apart. Thin to stand 4 to 6 inches apart when the seedlings have six to eight true leaves. The thinnings make good eating in a tossed salad. For a continuous supply of the leaves, sow small batches every few weeks.

Growing needs. Frequent feedings with diluted fertilizer are better than a lot all at once. Water plants with half-strength fish emulsion or other liquid fertilizer after planting and after harvest, or every three to four weeks. Good moisture levels are important, as dry conditions encourage plants to go to seed. Water plants in containers two or three times a week; once a week in the garden.

How to Harvest

For leaves. You can start to crop the leaves when plants are about 6 inches high. Frequent cutting encourages production of more leaves and delays the formation of seeds. To store the fresh leaves, wash in cold water, drain thoroughly, and wrap in a paper towel. Store in a plastic bag in the refrigerator. Some people prefer to place stems in a jar of water in the refrigerator; this works well if you can keep from tipping over the jar.

For seeds. To harvest seeds, watch to see when the first seedpods turn golden brown. If all the seeds are allowed to ripen fully on the plant, the pods will shatter, scattering the seeds, and you'll lose most of your crop. Instead, as soon as the first seedpods are dry, pull up the whole plant, put it in a paper bag, and hang it in a warm, dry place. The bags catch the ripening seeds in the bottom and also keep the plant clean. Rub the round seedpods between your hands to release the curved seeds within.

Unusual weather conditions can hasten maturity considerably. Keep an eye on your plants. They may surprise you by going to seed much earlier than expected.

Varieties

Almost any seed catalog that offers herb seeds lists cilantro/coriander. Catalogs that specialize in Asian vegetables may list it as Chinese parsley. If you grow this for its leaves, look for varieties described as slow to bolt. These give you a longer season of harvest before going to seed.

Varieties to look for: Asia Choice, Glory TW, Slow Bolt Winner.

FRESH LEAVES. Cilantro leaves are best when young and tender:

- Fresh leaves add zest and a touch of the unexpected to salads.

- Mince and sprinkle leaves over sliced and buttered Jerusalem artichokes.

- Fill hard-boiled egg halves with a mix of yolks blended with a little sesame oil and minced cilantro.

IN COOKED DISHES. Add cilantro toward the end of the cooking cycle.

- The Chinese make a particularly delectable beef stew, simmered with vegetables and seasoned with five spice powder and cilantro.

- Add cilantro to lamb stew during the last 20 minutes of cooking.

SEEDS. The flavor of the seeds is spicy citrus-orange with a touch of hot lime. The ground seeds are commonly used to flavor breads, puddings, and pastries, but don't limit your use of the seeds to sweet dishes. They are one of the spices most widely used in Indian curries, and their unique flavor is highly regarded in all Indian cookery.

- Incorporate in a vanilla blancmange with a thin orange slice or a garnish of minced orange mint.

- In Scandinavian countries, the seeds are often crushed and mixed with flour to make special breads. This custom may have found its way north from ancient Greece, where the seeds were ground up along with the flour for bread dough.

- Simmer crushed seeds in chicken broth for 2 or 3 minutes. Strain the broth and use to cook rice pilaf. If serving this with a chicken curry, chop up 2 or 3 oranges and a lemon and cook them along with the rice, stirring when the rice is half done to mix the fruit evenly throughout.

Mitsuba

SAN YE, SAN IP

Cryptotaenia canadensis ssp. *japonica*
(color photo, page xiv)

I have often thought it would be fun to plant a corner of an herb garden with all the different parsleys. I would have Italian or flat-leaved parsley, curly parsley, Hamburg parsley, cilantro (Chinese parsley), and mitsuba (Japanese parsley). The last two aren't really parsley, but I would stretch the point for the sake of an interesting garden.

Mitsuba is now classified as a sub-species of a North American plant; the two are almost identical. Honewort, or wild chervil (*Cryptotaenia canadensis*), grows wild from southern Canada to the southern United States. The American Indians ate it, and the Swedish plant explorer Peter Kalm wrote that the French Canadians were inordinately fond of it in soup. The Japanese recognized the value of mitsuba and put it under cultivation. Today it is widely grown, and it's slowly becoming available in this country.

Appearance

Mitsuba adds interest to the garden as a foliage plant. It looks a bit like flat-leaved Italian parsley, but the toothed leaflets are larger. They grow in groups of three and create a nice texture. Its flowers are small, white, and umbrella-shaped (typical of this family of plants). Garden books tell you that the flowers appear at the top of the plant, but don't be surprised if flowers appear an inch or two above the soil surface when the seeds are ripening at the top. This is a second flowering.

The seedpods are always described as long and ribbed, but "long" is relative. They're about ¼ inch long at most.

How to Grow

Getting started. Mitsuba is reasonably hardy and can be planted as early as the ground can be worked. If you grow it in a pot indoors over the winter, harden it off before you move the pot outside or transplant it.

Outdoors, it's best to plant mitsuba as an annual. You may find that it self-sows from year to year. It's not particularly fussy about soil. It will thrive in a moist, shady place, so save your sunny areas for plants that won't settle for less.

Planting. Sow seeds ½ inch deep and 2 inches apart; thin to 4 inches (eat the thinnings). Unlike the true parsley, mitsuba is not difficult to germinate and quickly shows a bit of green if you keep its planting site moist.

Growing needs. For the best crop, plant successively every three to four weeks and harvest the entire plant when you want to use it. Leave a few plants to go to seed for next season's crop. If possible, grow in partial to moderate shade. If you grow mitsuba in full sun, the leaves may turn yellow and look unhealthy. If this should happen, remove the discolored leaves and use only the new green.

Mature plants need steady moisture; don't let the soil dry out. When plants are about 1½ feet tall, side-dress with a small amount of balanced fertilizer or diluted liquid fertilizer. Avoid making the soil too rich. At the halfway mark, water is more important than fertilizer, so concentrate on the watering.

How to Harvest

For leaves. If you have a number of plants, you can gather leaves without disturbing the growth of the parent plant; seed production will continue undisturbed. Or pull the entire plant after about four weeks. If you wait until maturity (60 to 90 days) you can harvest the seeds *and* the roots. I generally take some of the plant at each stage; it's like having three different plants in the garden.

For seeds. If you let it flower, the small white blossoms will quickly turn to seed. To gather the caraway-shaped seeds, cut the whole stem to within 2 inches of the base. The part that remains in the ground will start to grow again. Dry on a sheet of paper or paper towel to hold the seeds as they dry and fall off. Dry thoroughly to store for next year's crop for an endless supply of this useful herb.

Varieties

Look for this plant in catalogs under "mitsuba," the Japanese name. However, in American edible-plant guides, wild chervil, or honewort, is sometimes mistakenly called mitsuba.

The seeds you buy may turn out to be different varieties. Some varieties have a slender white stem, some green. Sometimes the stems are hollow, sometimes not. They all taste much the same, so you can't go wrong.

— CULINARY USES —

Mitsuba is usually said to be celery-flavored, but I think it tastes more like Italian parsley, with a stronger flavor than curly parsley. Grow it and taste a leaf yourself; you will soon find many uses for this unique herb. The whole plant is edible — seeds, leaves, stem, and small roots — but save some seeds to plant next spring. Use the leaves and stems both raw and cooked:

- Mitsuba leaves are good in a mixed green salad with Bibb or leaf lettuce, or perhaps Chinese cabbage, also in cucumber salad.

- Simmer leaves briefly in clear chicken broth.

- Stir-fry leaves with mushrooms and shrimp.

- Mince and toss leaves with cooked vegetables.

- Add minced leaves to canapés of egg, shrimp, fish, or pâté.

- Add minced leaves to carrot or zucchini bread. A tablespoon or two gives flavor and aroma to the whole loaf.

- For a thoroughly English treat with an Asian flavor, make cucumber sandwiches on thinly sliced rye bread and butter, and garnish with minced mitsuba.

- Blanch roots for 5 minutes, then sauté in sesame oil, or boil together with root vegetables such as potatoes or parsnips.

Watercress

Xi Yang Choy, Sai Yeung Tsoi

Nasturtium officinale

(color photo, page xv)

Watercress grew wild throughout most of the ancient world except the Americas. This crisp, pungent herb became so popular that it was taken everywhere and was introduced to this continent, where it escaped to grow along brooks and steams throughout North and South America.

The Romans ate large quantities of watercress, partly because it was thought to prevent hair from falling out. The Greeks regarded it as a cure for insanity and also for drunkenness. (It was always served at large banquets.)

While watercress has long been gathered in the wild, it's no longer so easy to do. The plants are much harder to find, and even apparently clean streams may be polluted. You're better off growing your own. Nothing could be easier. If you grow it indoors, watercress is a good year-round vegetable.

Appearance

Watercress is a dark green, small-leaved plant usually sold in dripping bunches in the produce section of the supermarket. Never buy or use any that's turning yellow; it's good only for the compost heap.

How to Grow

Getting started. You can plant water-cress anytime, though most sources recommend starting seeds in early spring. Watercress must have wet feet and prefers *cool* water; as long as that's provided, it won't pay much attention to air temperatures. (If you run into a really hot spell, drop an ice cube into the water.)

Planting. You can grow watercress either from seeds or sprigs. Sow seeds on the surface of moist soil and just barely cover with more soil. If you're starting seeds indoors or planning to grow this indoors, mix a little limestone as well as some fertilizer into the soil before planting. Stand the pot or other seed container in another container of water (shallow or deep, doesn't matter).

To plant sprigs, I start watercress by buying a good, fresh bunch of water-cress in the market. I root the stems in water or soil, whichever happens to be more convenient at the time. It's easy. Remove any leaves that would lie under the soil or below the water line. Place in a glass of water, or poke all the little pieces of jointed stem into the soil so that the joint is covered by soil. They form roots in a few days and can then be transplanted into a permanent pot of moist soil with a bit of the stem out in the air. Remove any leaves that

turn yellow, and discard any stems that don't root. Once you've got it growing, you can easily get more stock by taking cuttings from the plants and rooting them in water or soil.

Growing needs. Watercress can be planted outside as long as you have a spot that stays moist all the time. It does best in high shade (a term for no sun but plenty of light). If you don't have the right conditions for growing

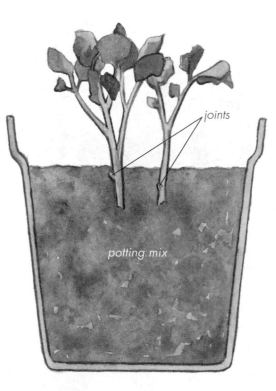

To root watercress, cut stems, remove leaves below soil or water line, and place in a glass of water or poke the pieces into soil, so the joints are covered.

it in the ground, grow it in a pot either indoors or out. I grow it on my porch in the summer and on a kitchen window-sill in the winter. It helps to have it near the sink because it needs fresh water once a day in the winter, twice a day in the summer. Empty yesterday's water out of the dish and fill it with fresh water run through the top of the pot.

Wider containers gives you a larger crop, since watercress spreads out into whatever space you give it. Put a layer of gravel or moss in the bottom of the pot to keep the soil from washing out through the drainage holes.

Occasional feeding and liming are necessary, because changing the water gradually leaches out the nutrients. Fertilize with quarter-strength liquid fertilizer every couple of weeks. I add a little limestone about once a month.

How to Harvest

Harvest watercress whenever you please. Don't let it flower, though. If it blooms, and especially if it goes to seed, it will be too bitter to be good eating. It matures in about 60 days from seeds. I never plant seeds, only stems, so mine can be picked in about 10 days.

Varieties

Generally only one variety is available. Look under cress as well as watercress in the index of seed catalogs and Web sites. There are several other plants called cress with a similar peppery flavor, including upland cress *(Barbarea verna)* and several varieties of a species that's popular in Europe, *Lepidum sativum*. These are grown in soil or sprouted the same way as bean sprouts.

DID YOU KNOW?

In addition to vitamin C, watercress is an excellent source of vitamin A. It has almost three times as much calcium as broccoli and is a valuable source of vitamin E, iron, and folate. If you use watercress regularly in place of lettuce, you'll add appreciably to your intake of vitamins and minerals. All this, and it's delicious, too.

Once you get started eating watercress, you'll think of many, many ways to use it.

SANDWICHES. Watercress makes great sandwiches. Cream cheese, cucumber, and watercress on whole-wheat bread is cool, crisp, and flavorful. Or substitute blue cheese blended with yogurt. Use watercress in sandwiches in packed lunches or for a picnic; the watercress won't go limp on a hot day the way lettuce will.

SOUPS. Make an unusual garnish for a hot or cold soup by whipping lightly salted cream and folding in finely chopped watercress. Cream of watercress soup is a real delight and very quick to prepare. Put the watercress in a blender with chicken stock, ginger, yogurt, and salt and pepper to taste. Blend very briefly, then heat to just under the boiling point. Serve hot or cold, with sprigs of fresh watercress as a garnish.

SALADS. Add sprigs of watercress to a mixed green salad or a plate of sliced tomatoes fresh from your garden, the whole lightly dressed with vinaigrette — very refreshing on a hot day.

CHINESE-STYLE. Since the Chinese tend not to use raw vegetables (unless they've been pickled) watercress is often fried. To make this, quickly stir-fry ginger and garlic in peanut oil, then add watercress, a few tablespoons of chicken stock, a little sherry, and some soy sauce, and continue stir-frying for another minute. Thicken with cornstarch and serve immediately as a hot vegetable.

JAPANESE-STYLE. Use watercress for tempura as the Japanese do.

Sesame

ZHI MA, CHIH MA

Sesamum indicum (formerly *S. orientale*)

(color photo, page xv)

Today sesame seeds are used primarily to produce an expensive oil; even in China this oil is used sparingly because of its cost. Oil from the toasted seeds is an important flavoring agent. The seeds, both raw and toasted, are used in the cookery of many lands.

In the *Arabian Nights* story of Ali Baba and the forty thieves, the fabulous treasure cave could be entered only by uttering two magic words: "Open sesame!" When Ali Baba spoke these words in a clear, firm voice, the cave opened and he was able to enter and gather untold riches. When as a child I read this story, I didn't attach any significance to the ritual; "sesame" had a good ring to it, and we used it in games and jokes. It's still an expression for a magic formula for anything literally or figuratively hard to open. Only later did I learn the author had simply used a common charm that he knew would be familiar to his readers.

Natives of the East Indies called sesame "thunderbolt" because they believed it held the power to open secret hiding places. Supposedly this derives from the way the seedpods burst open when ripe. In ancient Greece, sesame was a plant sacred to Hecate, goddess of the underworld and of witchcraft, and many spells depended on its use.

Sesame may be the most ancient of all herbs or spices. The oil extracted from it was known in the Euphrates valley as early as 1600 B.C.E.; it is also mentioned in Egyptian writings of about that period. It is apparently native to both Asia and Africa. Its use spread throughout Asia, where butter and olive oil never became popular, and it served both culinary and cosmetic purposes. It came to the American colonies along with African slaves and adapted well to the climate of Texas and other southern states. Wherever cotton grows well, sesame is a good commercial crop, and it has gone native in some areas. In the South, it was sometimes called "benne" or "bene," a name of African origin.

Appearance

Like so many of the plants in this book, sesame is ornamental and deserves a place in the garden for that reason alone. The plant stands about 3 feet high and is very erect. Depending on the variety, the flowers range in color from pink and deep pink (*Sesamum alatum*) to lavender-pink or white (*S. indicum*). They are large and prominent, something like foxglove in shape, and grow along the stem, opening in sequence from bottom to top.

The seeds are generally grayish or tannish to light cream, but black sesame seeds are highly regarded too. The pods are quite large; each one contains about 80 seeds. Since there are usually over a hundred pods to a plant, you can get a good crop from just a few plants.

How to Grow

Getting started. Sesame is a warm-weather plant and can't be set out until all danger of frost has passed. It requires a fairly long growing season, as plants take 90 to 150 days after sowing to reach maturity. In cold climates, start it indoors at least a month before setting out. (See page 201.) Wait until soil is quite warm (about a month after the last spring frost) to set out plants.

Planting. Sow seeds ½ inch deep and 1 inch apart. If you plant in rows, they should stand about 3 feet apart. The seedlings (which can be eaten) should be thinned to stand 8 inches apart when about 6 inches tall.

Growing needs. Sesame requires full sun. Though it will grow in almost any soil, for superlative results plant it in a good vegetable-garden soil and dig in compost and a moderate amount of balanced fertilizer before planting. Plants need steady moisture until they begin flowering to assure good yields. Once plants reach the flowering stage they tolerate drought.

How to Harvest

Harvesting the seeds is a little tricky for two reasons. First, the seedpods burst open when ripe, so if you don't gather them in time the seeds will fall on the ground. Second, they don't all mature at the same time.

The timing depends on catching the first seeds to ripen. Leaves and stems start to turn color when they mature, and you want to catch them before this happens. Watch the bottom seeds, since they ripen from the bottom to the top. When the bottom seeds seem to be turning tan and the top seeds seem full-sized though still green, cut the whole plant and put it upside down in a paper bag. Hang the bag with a thumb-tack in the garage or some other warm, dry place and let the seeds shatter and shell themselves for you into the bottom of the bag.

Varieties

Look for sesame seeds under "herbs" in most catalogs. Black sesame seeds are a different variety of *Sesamum indicum.* Japanese sources call unhulled white sesame seed *shiro-goma* and black sesame seed *juro-goma.*

For commercial growers, a variety has been developed that doesn't shatter so easily and that matures at about the same time all along the stem. This needn't concern the home gardener, who can harvest the plants as soon as the first seeds become ripe.

Varieties to look for: Black Seed, White Seed.

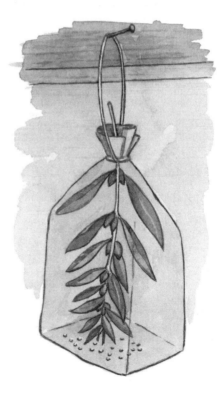

Hang plant upside down in a paper bag so that seeds can fall to the bottom as they mature and dry.

Each sesame plant produces an enormous quantity of seeds so you can easily grow enough for a year's use from just a small sowing. You'll save money, too, because sesame seeds are expensive unless you buy them in bulk. The seeds are delicious both raw and toasted. (It isn't necessary to toast seeds on dishes that will be baked since they will be toasted in the cooking process.) When you become familiar with their taste, you'll invent ways to include them in everyday recipes. Here are some suggestions for use:

- They are an excellent snack.
- Use as a garnish for salads.
- Add to stir-fry dishes.
- Sprinkle on boiled carrots or beets.
- Press into pie crust for a peach pie.

HOW TO TOAST SESAME SEEDS

Most cookbooks tell you to toast sesame seeds in a frying pan over medium heat until the seeds start to jump like popcorn. I don't like this method because you have to keep shaking the pan and stirring the seeds to keep them from burning. I prefer the following method.

1. Put them in a single layer on a cookie sheet in a low oven (200°F to 250°F).
2. Toast for 3 to 5 minutes until golden brown. Keep a sharp eye on them so that they don't burn.
3. Leave them on the sheet to cool.
4. When completely cool, store in a spice jar or other tight container.

Note: Don't toast them all; the raw seeds are delicious and useful, and they keep indefinitely.

TAHINI. It's easy to grind sesame seeds into tahini, a paste something like peanut butter, only much more delicate. Tahini lends itself to a wide variety of uses in salad dressings, candies, pastries, casseroles, and so forth. You can make tahini in the blender with the addition of a little sesame oil (the same way you make homemade peanut butter), or purchase a Japanese grinder designed for this purpose that is made of plastic and easy to clean and store.

TOASTED OIL. A few tablespoons of this flavorful oil added in the Chinese manner at the end of a stir-fry or sauté dish impart a delightfully nutty flavor to the entire contents. Used in braising delicate vegetables such as fennel, Belgian endive, or even celery, it creates a company dish in just a few minutes of cooking.

SESAME PLANT LEAVES. The plant is edible in many stages:

- When young, the leaves can be gathered and used sparingly in tossed salads.

- Simmer leaves until tender and season with a few drops of soy sauce and sesame oil.

- In the South, the leaves were traditionally used to make a beverage considered both soothing and beneficial. To make this, whirl young leaves in the blender with a quantity of water and let stand about 5 minutes, then pour over ice cubes.

DID YOU KNOW?

Sesame seeds and oil are good for you. The seeds are rich in calcium, magnesium, iron, phosphorous, thiamine, zinc, and fiber. In addition, the seeds and oil are considered particularly desirable because they contain monounsaturated and polyunsaturated fats. They are good sources of antioxidants, which explains why sesame oil lasts a long time without turning rancid. The oil is relatively stable at high temperatures, making it a good choice for frying.

Ginger

JIANG, GEUNG

Zingiber officinale

(color photo, page xiv)

If you have a spice shelf, chances are that ground ginger is on it. Everywhere in the world it's one of the most popular and widely used spices. Many varieties of ginger grow wild from China to the United States, but the finest varieties originated in the East Indies and India. In Japan, it is called shoga.

Its use spread rapidly; by the Middle Ages, it was known throughout the civilized world. When it reached the West Indies, it found the perfect climate. Jamaican ginger is known, even in China, as one of the finest gingers grown anywhere, and it is a principal export of the West Indies.

By the fourteenth century, ginger was so well liked in England that its consumption ranked second only to pepper. Shakespeare, always quick to reflect the popular taste, speaks of it as the ultimate love offering when he writes, in *Love's Labour's Lost*, "An I had but one penny in the world, thou shouldst have it to buy ginger-bread."

Appearance

Ginger roots are a pleasant tan color with a smooth, woody look. They grow in a knobby sort of way. The ginger plant is reedy-looking and grows about 2 to 3 feet tall. Glossy, bright green leaves are narrow and up to 6 inches long. It's sometimes called "the queen of the greenhouse" because of its brilliant, showy flowers. Some gardeners grow it as an ornamental, never realizing the buried treasure they have beneath the soil.

How to Grow

Getting started. Ginger usually "rests" during the winter months, so plant it early in the spring. The earlier you can start it indoors, the greater the maturity of the root you harvest in the fall, but you must wait for really warm weather to move it outside. In warmer parts of Florida, it can be planted in February or early March; in cooler climates, start it in January and plant it outdoors in late spring when all danger of frost has passed. Dig it up in the fall before there's any chance of frost. If it's still growing strongly, you can pot it and let it finish growing indoors. If this sounds like too much of a bother, harvest the delicious immature roots instead.

Planting. The easiest source for ginger root is your local market. It's normally available all year round, but not all roots will sprout. Buy a large, clean, firm root that's not discolored or spongy. Cut into 1- to 2-inch pieces; each piece should have at least one "eye" or knob. Put the pieces 2 to 3 inches deep in a 6-inch pot of rich potting soil and keep soil moist.

After two weeks, if no shoots have appeared dig up the roots. If they look the same as when you planted them, wash them off, dry them thoroughly, and put aside to use. If small, pronounced ivory bumps have developed, then replant — these are the beginnings of shoots and show that the root is alive.

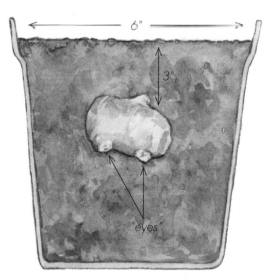

Place a large, clean, firm ginger root with at least one "eye" about 2 to 3 inches deep in a pot of rich potting soil.

Growing needs. When you replant, add a tablespoon of time-release fertilizer and work well into the soil. Continue to keep soil moist at all times, but be sure drainage is good; this plant does not like wet feet. Until the shoots are a couple of inches high, provide two hours of sun a day but not more. Then gradually acclimate plants to more sun. Transplant into a larger pot whenever the plant fills its container. Wait to move outdoors until nights are no longer cold. Ginger does not like wind. If grown on a terrace, a windbreak should be provided; otherwise grow it in a sunny corner well protected from wind. If you're growing a lot of ginger, space the plants 16 inches apart in rows 24 inches apart.

As the plant develops, numerous reedy shoots will grow and form an interesting clump. In the sixth or seventh month after planting, flower stalks will grow out of the clump. Ginger is a heavy feeder and benefits from frequent applications of diluted liquid fertilizer.

The plant's normal cycle is to die down over the winter. Dig up the roots and store in sand until spring. If you wish to keep the plant going in the house, give it a resting period. Withhold water and fertilizer and allow plants to go dormant for two months. You can force winter blooms by planting it in a pot about nine months before you want the flowers; it will subsequently go dormant on its usual schedule.

DID YOU KNOW?

If you like to cook highly spiced food (whether Chinese or Indian), always include ginger among your spices. This is the secret ingredient of those lands; ginger has a soothing effect on the digestive tract and counteracts the other hot spices used. One of the chief uses of ginger in the Far East is as an aid to digestion. Try it for yourself. You'll find that nibbling on a piece of crystallized ginger relieves discomfort after a too-heavy meal. In the United States, ginger ale is frequently recommended for nausea and other stomach disorders.

In addition to its medicinal value, ginger is a good source of vitamin C (also magnesium and potassium). The wise Chinese took pots of ginger with them on long sea voyages to prevent scurvy, and this practice was considerably before the British navy learned to achieve the same result with limes.

How to Harvest

For shoots. The shoots are delicious and can be cut anytime after they are 3 inches high. The roots will continue to sprout if you don't take too many shoots, so this cropping will do the plant no harm. A famous Japanese delicacy is a condiment made by marinating ginger shoots in a blend of vinegar, sugar, and sesame oil.

For "green ginger." To harvest the roots, dig away enough soil to expose them. Cut off the rosy-pink baby roots for a special treat; these are known as "green ginger." Look for them three to four months after you've planted the root. These juvenile roots are recognizably gingery but so mild and delicate you'll think it's a different plant. The flavor and the "heat" of ginger are the result of two different substances; the immature root has not yet developed the *gingerin* that makes ginger "hot." These baby roots are sufficient reason for including ginger somewhere in the home garden or windowsill.

For mature roots. Once plants have died back and the stem has withered, the mature root can be dug up whole. You can also gather one joint at a time from plants that are still growing. When harvesting the mature root, always leave the plant enough to grow on.

Varieties

In addition to the variety of ginger we commonly use, there are many other gingers grown in China, Japan, and India. One of them tastes like bergamot, another is lemon-scented. Not all members of the ginger family are edible, so don't sample an ornamental ginger without carefully checking whether it can be eaten.

Ginger is equally good in main dishes and desserts, hot or cold, in salads or stews. It does wonders for roasts and soups, and in beverages. Ginger lends zest to many bland meat dishes. It eliminates the fishy odors of seafood without spoiling the delicate natural flavors of the fish.

A piece of ginger keeps in the refrigerator for at least a week. Don't put it in the vegetable compartment, where the moisture encourages mold. Store in plastic wrap on a shelf. For longer storage, keep a piece of the root in the freezer; grate as much as you need while still frozen. Or it will keep almost indefinitely if you put the root in a small jar, cover with sherry or vodka, and refrigerate.

WITH RICE. A simple rice pilaf cooked with ginger, scallions, and sautéed garlic becomes a company dish.

AS A HOT DRINK. On a cold wintry afternoon offer guests a nineteenth-century English tavern drink. Sprinkle a little freshly ground ginger on top of a mug of ale (not beer), mull with a hot poker, and serve.

GINGERBREAD. That old standby gingerbread is still beloved by both children and adults. Try serving it with whipped cream spiked with a bit of finely minced, candied ginger.

RAW GINGER. Use raw ginger with discretion:

- Grate into a dressing for a fruit salad.
- A thin slice added to honeyed hot tea makes a healthful and delicious beverage.
- Substitute grated ginger whenever dried ground ginger is called for, using about half the quantity indicated.

MARINATED GINGER. In Japan the baby roots (green ginger) are marinated briefly in rice vinegar and sugar. Pickled ginger is called "sour ginger" in Chinese (in Mandarin, *suan jiang*; in Cantonese, *syun geung*).

7

THE CHINESE WATER GARDEN

**VIOLET-STEMMED TARO • WATER CHESTNUT •
CHINESE LOTUS • ARROWHEAD**

Some of the essential plants for Chinese cooking don't grow in soil but in water. If you want to grow your own water chestnuts, you'll have to venture into the world of water gardening. If you've always wanted a water garden but thought you didn't have the room, you'll be happy to hear that you can have a beautiful one in an area no larger than a portable washtub — in fact, you can actually have one *in* a washtub.

A container water garden is the easiest kind of container gardening. It's particularly good for the weekend gardener because it requires practically no upkeep. You don't have to nurse and transplant seedlings. You rarely have to water (except to top up during dry spells), you never need to mulch, and you only fertilize occasionally. There are no weeds. Most water plants aren't winter hardy in much of North America, so growing them in containers simplifies winter care. Furthermore, all the lovely water plants described in this chapter are deliciously edible and are common, everyday vegetables in Asian cuisine. Your garden will be a delightful conversation piece, can go in any sunny location you please, and can even be moved around if necessary.

Water gardens can be as small as a 5-gallon container or as large as a pond. Or they can be something in between, such as three 25-gallon tubs artistically deployed over a large patio. The room you have — whether it's a city terrace, a rooftop, a balcony, or a backyard — and your enthusiasm are the only limits. A sun deck, front doorstep, or breezeway will be enhanced with a container of these attractive plants. Just keep in mind that these plants require full sun.

This small, easy-to-maintain water garden contains arrowhead (A), colocasia (B), Chinese lotus (C), and water chestnut (D).

What You Need to Get Started

Making your first water garden a small, very limited project gives you a chance to see how you like water gardening, whether you have a wet green thumb, and whether you want to grow these particular vegetables. I should warn you, however, that it tends to be addictive; one small tub is likely to grow into a much more elaborate project. Although water gardening may look hard, it's actually so easy that the temptation is to undertake a little more each year. There isn't much danger that you'll be inundated with your crops; the danger is that you will be led to combine edible with ever more inedible but irresistibly beautiful water plants.

No matter whether you choose a container or an in-the-ground pond, you should consult water-garden suppliers. They can provide advice as to what will work best for your climate and conditions, what kind of containers are available, how much they cost, and what you'll need for the garden you have in mind. If you're completely at sea, they'll even plan a complete container or pond garden for you. If you prefer to do it all yourself, you'll find it easier than planning the usual vegetable garden.

IN-GROUND WATER GARDENS

If you have the room and the site, you may prefer a permanent pool for your Chinese water garden. An in-ground water garden can be a charming, small woodland pool in very little space. Water gardening is what you make it; whatever suits your lifestyle can be created with very little fuss. Although there are winter-hardy water plants, these vegetables are not among them. If you live in an area where the temperatures go below freezing, an in-the-ground water garden of edible plants is more work than a tub garden. You need to lift and store the plants over the winter, unless you can winterize the pond with a cover plus deep mulch to keep it from freezing.

SITING. Siting a permanent pond must be done more carefully than placing a container that can be moved if you should change your mind. If unsure of your own ability to integrate this feature into your present setting, consult with a landscape architect. If you feel you can do it yourself, make rough sketches of different sites to help you get the feel of them. (You don't have to be an artist for these.) Check your local building codes as well.

It's important to take into account how your present plantings will look when they mature several years from now. A small tree that grows into a large one can turn a sunny site into a shady dell — a poor site for a water garden. Think also of the uses of the area around the pond. A pond is a pleasant place for contemplation; it may not be at its best next to the kids' play area.

WINTERIZING. Winterizing is greatly simplified by planting all plants in individual containers. If your pond includes hardy ornamentals, those containers stay; the tender ones lift right out without arduous digging. Your pond will appear undisturbed, and in the spring the edible plants can be put back in place with comparatively little bother.

What You Need to Get Started

Anything that holds water and is big enough for what you want to grow can be used for a water garden. Plastic or galvanized-iron containers are usually recommended (although an occasional water-garden expert frowns on metal containers). These can be set inside something more decorative, such as a half-barrel, if you feel they're not sufficiently attractive. Something as simple as a washtub or a child's wading pool works surprisingly well. Water-garden suppliers have all sizes of tubs as well as a number of free-form pools, so you don't have to hunt around if you don't want to.

I picked up an old galvanized-iron washtub years ago and it became a container garden for peanuts, sweet potatoes, and Chinese flowering cabbages. Still in good condition, it's now just the thing for a small water garden. A can of spray paint keeps the outside in harmony with its surroundings, and the two side handles make it easy to move around as landscaping inclinations change.

If I wanted, I could use the tub as an in-the-ground pond, fitting it into a small hole dug in the lawn; the edges could be hidden with a little soil and suitable plantings. The possibilities of water container gardening are limited only by your imagination.

Pots for Individual Plants

Within your main container place individual containers, each one holding one plant or clump. The plastic pots used for water gardens differ from those you use for houseplants; they are shaped for greater stability and may have perforated sides so water can move freely in and out of the pot. Get these from a water-garden supplier; the pots are inexpensive and long-lasting. Square containers take up less room than round. You can use them for everything but lotus, the root of which grows in circles and requires a round container.

These indiviual containers offer several advantages. They use much less soil than you'd need to cover the entire bottom to a sufficient depth. It's much easier to make changes when all you have to do is lift out a container. Even a small tub is much harder to change around if the plants are buried. Also, a muddy bottom tends to promote murky water, especially since the ecology of water plants requires fish, and their movement tends to stir up mud. Fish like to dart in and out of the mud, stirring it up even more.

Even the most carefully planned water garden needs an occasional cleaning. With container gardening, you just set aside the individual containers; moving buried plants or trying to clean around them would be quite a chore.

Finally, if you live in a climate where the temperature drops below freezing (and this includes most of the United States) you must take out your plants for the winter. This procedure is simple and easy with containers.

Note: Redwood discolors the water and should not be used either for the main tub or the individual pots. If you like the look of redwood, line it with a slightly smaller plastic container.

Supports

The plant descriptions on pages 156 to 168 include the depth at which to grow each plant. If you are growing it in a pond or in a container that's deeper than the recommended depth, you'll need some sort of support under your pot to raise it to the right height. A rock, an upside-down pot, or an old plastic storage container upside down — whatever achieves the desired depth — will work. If you're combining plants in a large tub, try various supports to give you a pleasing arrangement and allow plants to grow at their preferred depths.

Soil and Fertilizer

Neither the standard soil mix nor the Cornell Mix described on page 177 works well for water gardens. It floats and makes a mess. Water gardens require a heavy soil. Purchase a planting medium designed for use in water gardens; it contains some type of clay instead of peat moss. If you have good garden soil that contains a high proportion of clay, you can use that, and there are some aquatic potting mixes designed to be mixed with garden soil.

You also need special fertilizer for water gardens. Ordinary gardening types promote algae, and those formulated for water gardens are designed to minimize algae. Aquatic planting media and fertilizer are available from any water-garden supplier.

Mix half a pot of this soil with the amount of fertilizer recommended on the product package and put this mixture in the bottom half of your pot. Add more unamended soil so the pot is about three-quarters full, then set in the plant. Add more soil to cover the roots, but don't cover the crown (growing tips) of the plant. Firm with your fingers. To keep the soil from washing out of the pot, cover the top with ½ inch of gravel or sand. This is the basic procedure for potting all water plants. Specific cultural directions, where they differ from this, are given under each vegetable.

Plant Sources

Water plants are sold as plants rather than seeds. Unless you have a nursery nearby that specializes in water gardens, you'll have to order plants from a specialty supplier (see Appendix).

Some suppliers may be a baffled at the thought of growing these plants for food. Others are completely familiar with this use of their plants and can be very helpful, so don't hesitate to ask them for advice.

Submerged Oxygenating Plants (SOP)

Every kind of gardening has a few terms peculiar to it; water gardening is no exception. One of the terms you must understand is SOP, which stands for "submerged oxygenating plants." Unless you want to invest in (and maintain) expensive filters, you can't have a successful water garden without including these plants to maintain clear water and a healthful environment. SOPs consume most of the carbon dioxide in the water and help control algae by absorbing mineral salts in the water. The plants provide a friendly spot for fish who depend on them for refuge and for the oxygen they produce under the water. Again, they are available from water-garden suppliers.

If you're using containers, the SOP should be planted one-third deep in the center of the container. (In a pond with a muddy bottom, you plant SOPs just by dropping the cuttings into the pond.) The recommended rate of planting is two bunches per one 7- to 12-inch-diameter pot, 3 to 5 inches deep. Allow approximately one bunch for every 2 square feet of water surface for containers. (In larger ponds the requirements may be somewhat different.)

INVASIVE ALERT!

Some of the plants commonly used as submerged oxygenating plants (SOPs) are noxious invasives. Eurasian watermilfoil (*Myriophyllum spicatum*) is on the most-wanted list of invasive plants that clog waterways, interfering with swimming and boating. Though fanwort (*Cabomba caroliniana*) is native to the southeastern United States, it is considered an invasive in northeastern and northwestern states.

Suppliers often don't list the species of SOP they supply, so you may not know what you're getting. Assume it's an invasive plant. Never allow exotic plants (or fish) to enter a stream, a natural pond with an outlet, or other waterway. They are fine in your container water garden, as long as you dispose of them by composting or discarding with your garbage in a closed plastic bag.

Fish and Snails

In addition to SOPs, you have to add two other things to your water garden to keep it in proper balance: fish and snails. Fish act as natural insecticides, eating aphids, mosquito larvae, and other insects that come within their reach. A small tub with two bunches of SOPs does well with just two 4- to 5-inch fish. These can be ordinary goldfish or Japanese koi. These, too, are available from water-garden suppliers, as are snails. A local pet store may sell them also, but be sure to say they are for outdoor use (and get food and instructions for feeding them at the same time).

In severe winters, you should take in a few of the goldfish to guarantee that you have some the following season. Goldfish are, however, amazingly hardy; they survive as long as the whole container doesn't freeze solid.

Snails take out the garbage. You need them in your pond to eat algae and debris. The usual recommendation is one snail for every 1 to 2 square feet of surface in your container.

Lotuses and Water Lilies

Unlike the lilies of the field, water lilies do toil and spin — or at least they serve a practical function as well as looking beautiful and being edible. One lotus or a medium to large water lily should be included for every square yard of surface area in your pond. Since a single Chinese lotus requires a 25-gallon container, small water gardens might have to settle for a purely ornamental (inedible) water lily. The lily pads shade the water surface and so help maintain the proper water temperature. They also help keep oxygen in the water; the oxygen collects on the underside of the pads and is prevented from escaping into the air. Oxygen is important to support the ecological balance.

Controlling Algae

Algae begins growing in any body of water that's congenial to them as soon as the weather gets warm. Since they turn the water an unattractive green, do whatever is necessary to keep your water sparkling clear and algae free. This is not difficult, but timing is important. At the first sign of green water — a common occurrence in the early weeks after planting — treat the water with a special preparation that water-garden suppliers sell for this purpose. Repeat whenever necessary to keep the water clear.

Some ingenious water gardener discovered that barley straw helps to keep ponds free of algae. You can buy "pillows" of barley straw designed for water gardens, and these may eliminate the need for treating your water.

Violet-Stemmed Taro

Yu Tou, Woo Chai
Colocasia esculenta 'Fontanesii'
(color photo, page xvi)

This lovely water plant originated in tropical America. Early on, it spread to Africa and then to Asia, where it escaped to grow in ponds and waterways. Now, it's an essential ingredient in authentic Asian cuisine.

You'll find other roots called taro, as explained on page 158. This can be especially confusing because they too are used in Asian cookery. This one also goes by the names black taro and black elephant ear.

Appearance

The violet-stemmed taro is grown mostly as an ornamental in this country, valued for its unusual foliage. The large arrow-shaped, blue-green leaves have violet edges. They grow up to 2 feet in length under ideal conditions on beautiful dark violet, almost black stems that rise about 2 feet above the water. The midribs and veins underneath the leaves are also violet. This taro rarely flowers, but the foliage is a picture in itself.

How to Grow

Getting started. Unlike lotus and water chestnut, this water plant doesn't need full sun. In warmer climates, it prefers light to partial shade, but it tolerates more sun in cooler areas. Taro is a bog plant and should have no more than 3 to 6 inches of water above its soil line. You may have to prop up your taro pot in most water containers to bring it to the proper depth.

Planting. The number of taro roots you can put in a pot depends upon the size of the pot. Figure one root for a 7-inch-diameter pot that's 5 inches deep. A pot 19 inches in diameter and 9 inches deep holds six roots. If you put more than one root in a pot, they should be spaced evenly apart.

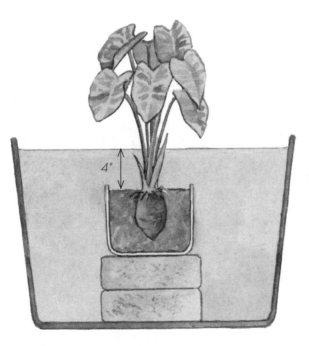

Set taro pot on bricks so that the soil surface is about 4" below the water line.

How to Harvest

The foliage will die down in the fall. Harvest the roots then; they're as mature as they'll get that season. If you intend to eat most of the roots, save the small offsets for next spring's plants.

Winter Storage

Taro tubers are hardy to about 32°F. Unless your winters stay above freezing, the tubers need to be lifted and stored for winter. To store in cold climates, remove the pots (with the offsets in them) from the container and turn them on their sides in a cool, moist, shady place — an unheated cellar is fine. It's important not to let the roots dry out, so check every so often to be sure the soil is moist.

In the spring, when the weather and water warms up, put the pots back in

DID YOU KNOW?

Raw taro (*Colocasia esculenta* and its cultivars) is toxic because it contains calcium oxalate crystals. These are destroyed by cooking. Taro can also be made edible by soaking rhizomes in water overnight. Avoid tasting raw taro as you're preparing it because it will burn your tongue. Some people are even sensitive to handling raw taro. If you discover your skin is sensitive to it, wear rubber gloves when preparing it.

the water container and you're all set for another season. If you haven't eaten all the roots, they may have become too big for their original pots. In that case they should be repotted.

Varieties

Green taro (*Colocasia esculenta*), also simply called taro or dasheen, is similar but lacks the dramatic dark stems. The cultivar 'Illustris' is known as imperial taro; it has lighter green leaves with dark purple markings between veins.

Several other cultivars of this species are also available.

The Chinese name *woo chai* is also used for a related plant, blue taro (*Xanthosoma violacea*). It, too, has an edible tuber but doesn't grow in water. Like the *Colocasia* taros, it's grown as an ornamental. In the Caribbean, blue taro is also known as *malanga* and *yautia*. These names are used in some Chinese cookbooks prepared for Americans. If you grow your own taro, you'll know which one you are eating.

─ CULINARY USES ─

You can find taro root in the fresh-produce department of markets that cater to Spanish and Chinese consumers. The root is about the size of a large white potato, brownish with a rough, thick skin. It's not particularly attractive, but it turns into a delicious vegetable that some gourmets consider superior to our white potato.

INSTEAD OF POTATOES. Taro can be baked like a potato and served with a pat of butter. You can substitute taro in any potato recipe with good results; they're especially tasty in a good rich stew. Try taro pancakes. Make them just like potato pancakes; they're especially good with a spoonful of yogurt over them.

TRADITIONAL ASIAN-STYLE. Peel, slice, and cook until tender. Meanwhile make a dressing in your blender with toasted sesame seeds, rice vinegar, and a little sugar. Add enough water to make it slightly liquid, heat, and pour over the hot taro.

IN CUSTARD. To make this very popular taro dish, use coconut milk, 3 eggs, sugar, ½ cup mashed taro root, and lime juice, following any standard custard recipe.

Water Chestnut

MA TI, MA TAI

Eleocharis dulcis

(color photo, page xvi)

Anyone who's eaten Chinese food knows water chestnuts. Supermarkets carry them canned and packed in water. Unfortunately, canned water chestnuts are a pale version of the real thing; both crispness and flavor suffer in the canning process. With an edible water garden, you can have all the fresh water chestnuts you choose to grow. They are an exceptionally easy crop and multiply rapidly.

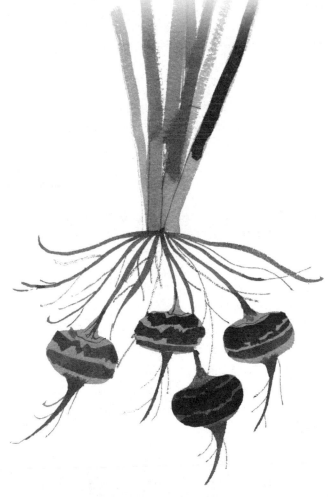

The Chinese have eaten water chestnuts for many centuries. The chestnuts are grown in large tanks as a single crop, or sometimes grown in rice paddies, since they don't interfere with the rice plants.

Aside from being good eating, Chinese water chestnuts make an attractive addition to a mixed water garden. Their tall, spiky foliage offers wonderful contrast to other water plants, and they combine well with most other water plants, including the lotus.

Appearance

Water chestnuts grow as erect clumps of green quills; the "leaves" are actually narrow tubular stems and grow to 3 feet tall. Though they look like a grass, they're in the sedge family; they and other *Eleocharis* species are called water rushes. Water chestnuts are not, of course, true nuts but edible roots (technically corms) with a distinctly nutty flavor, especially when freshly gathered.

The "chestnuts" form in the mud at the base of the stems. When fully mature, they're about the size of a walnut. They're covered with a tough brown skin.

How to Grow

Getting started. Water chestnuts require full sun and fairly rich soil to produce a decent crop. They are bog plants, so their containers should be set shallowly in your water container. The water surface should stand no more than 3 to 5 inches above the soil surface. Individual planters can range in size from 7 inches in diameter and 5 inches deep to 20 inches in diameter and 10 inches deep, depending on how many plants you want to grow and what else you want to grow with them. A 25-gallon container will produce about 30 to 40 mature chestnuts; smaller containers will produce proportionately fewer.

How to Harvest

Water chestnuts mature in about six months but can be gathered much sooner if your growing season is not that long, or if you'll settle for smaller "nuts."

Winter Storage

In climates where roots would freeze under water, they must be stored over winter. Remove the roots from the water (in their containers) and store in a cool, moist, shady place where they won't freeze. Lay the pots on their sides. Check every so often to be sure the soil has not dried out.

DID YOU KNOW?

You may have heard that water chestnuts are an invasive plant clogging lakes and other waterways throughout the eastern United States. Fortunately, that's an unrelated plant, though it shares the same common name. The troublesome one is the European water chestnut (*Trapa nutans*), a plant with rosettes of triangular leaves that float on the water.

Even if you're growing plants not known to be invasive, it's a good idea to be careful. Never dump exotic plants, seeds, or tubers (or fish!) into open bodies of water. Growing in containers is the safest way to raise exotic water plants, especially if you compost the tops at the end of the season.

Water chestnuts are prized for two characteristics: their nutty flavor and their crispness. They can be eaten both raw and cooked, but add toward the end of cooking so they don't lose their crispness. They should be peeled before slicing. Once peeled, store in water in the refrigerator, as the white flesh discolors quickly if exposed to air. If you need to keep peeled water chestnuts more than a day, change the water every 24 hours. (Unpeeled water chestnuts do not have to be stored in water.)

SALAD. Slice water chestnuts thin and add to a tossed salad with radishes and cucumbers; this makes one of the best salads ever.

STIR-FRY. For a good vegetarian stir fry, combine sliced water chestnuts with mushrooms, bamboo shoots, snow peas, bean sprouts, scallions, and taro root. Slice all the ingredients or cut into small pieces so they cook quickly, in about 5 minutes. Cook in stock seasoned with soy sauce, and thicken the gravy with cornstarch. If you like a hotter version, add a chili pepper and some grated fresh ginger. For meat eaters, cook shredded chicken or pork before adding the vegetables.

IN SAUCE. Make a sweet-and-sour sauce (rice vinegar and sugar) and cook water chestnuts along with bell peppers, celery, bamboo shoots, and Chinese cabbage. Like most Chinese recipes, once the vegetables are prepared, the cooking time is about 6 minutes.

SOUP. A clear soup garnished with a few thin slices of water chestnut is an authentic beginning to a Chinese meal, although it would work just as well before a roast beef dinner.

DID YOU KNOW?

In China, water-chestnut flour is a valued cooking ingredient, but you probably won't grow enough of your own chestnuts to use them in this way.

Chinese Lotus

Lian Ou, Lin Ngau

Nelumbo nucifera

(color photo, page xvi)

Several different species are called Egyptian lotus or sacred lotus, all represented in Egyptian art and architecture from earliest times. The Egyptian lotus (Nymphaea lotus) is actually a water lily and looks different from the Chinese or sacred lotus (Nelumbo nucifera).

Leaves of the Egyptian lotus rest on the water surface, and its flowers bloom close to the water on relatively short stems. Blossoms have the classic water lily shape with narrow pink-tinged white petals.

The blue cousin of this species, *Nymphaea caerulea,* was also called "lotus" and appears in ancient hieroglyphics. The Chinese lotus is the most desirable from a culinary standpoint. All three species grow wild in Egypt, so that accounts for some of the confusion.

Since ancient times the lotus has been revered throughout the Middle East, India, and Asia. It is a symbol of purity because it rises undefiled from the mud; as such it has been incorporated into the religions of many countries. Readers may be familiar with the "lotus position," the sitting position in which Buddhists meditate, with the legs crossed and each foot resting on the opposing thigh. Statues of Buddha frequently show him in this position.

Because the lotus displays all three stages of growth — bud, flower, and seedpod — simultaneously, it symbolizes the past, present, and future. This is sometimes illustrated in Japanese flower arrangements, with the past represented by a leaf that is past its prime or even decayed or worm-eaten, the present by a perfect leaf and flower, the future by a bud.

Lotus flowers are worth growing for their beauty alone; they're a wonderful ornament in the garden and beautiful in a vase. If you grow this showy flower and delicious vegetable, the problem will be not how to use it but how to grow enough for all the uses to which you'll wish to put it.

Appearance

The lotus is an exceptionally beautiful plant, among the loveliest of all water garden plants. It bears leaves and blooms on long stems, holding them well above the water. Buds, blossoms, and seedpods are striking in shape and beautiful. Buds take three days to open fully in a fascinating progression; they follow the sun during the day and close at night. Seedpod formation begins after the third day. Flowers are large, to 12 inches across in warm climates, with very wide petals. At one stage of the blossoming these look like an unfurling peony or rose. The leaves can reach 20 inches across. They are an elegant silvery blue-green and rise well above the water; the fragrant flowers grow even higher.

Lotus are perennials and hardy to Zone 4. With proper care, they'll give you years of pleasure — if you can keep from eating them all up.

The lotus rhizome looks something like a reddish brown banana joined in segments like a string of sausages (a mixed-up description, but apt). The flesh is light orange.

DID YOU KNOW?

The lotus of Greek mythology and Tennyson's famous poem is not the water plant, Chinese lotus (*Nelumbo nucifera*). It is generally believed to be a tree now known as jujube (*Ziziphus jujuba*). According to Greek mythology, eating the fruit of this tree caused you to while away your days in dreamy languor, forgetful of family, friends, and home. Fortunately (or unfortunately, as the case may be), the Chinese lotus does not have this effect.

How to Grow

Getting started. Chinese lotus should be grown in full sun. The more sun, the more freely it flowers. Less than full sun gives you some flowers, but plants do not make their full glorious show.

Your container must be round, because lotus roots grow in a circle. The minimum size container for a single lotus root is a bushel or 25 gallons. A single lotus root can grow as large as 4 feet long and 3 inches in diameter if you let it. The lotus is set the deepest of your water vegetables, so if it is grown with other plants, your main water container needs to be deep enough to accommodate the lotus. The main container needs to be 8 to 12 inches taller than the lotus container, as lotus plants need at least 6 but not more than 10 inches of warm water above the soil line. Fill the container with potting soil and fertilizer (see page 153 for advice).

Planting. Lotus plants are started from rhizomes rather than seeds. (You can grow new plants from seeds, but it's a very slow process.) Rhizomes are shipped from April to June, so get your order in early. When you receive the lotus rhizome from the water-garden supplier, one or more shoots are usually growing straight up, at right angles to the root.

Plant the rhizome horizontally, with the sprouts pointing upward at a slight angle; the end opposite the section with the sprouts should slant slightly downward. Plant 2 inches deep while still allowing the growing tips to stand about ¼ inch above the surface soil in the container.

Growing needs. Once planted, don't place in cold water or a situation where the water will get very cold. Once the plants are established, they will tolerate colder water, but they shouldn't start their growth under stress. Fertilize monthly during its growing season (approximately April to September).

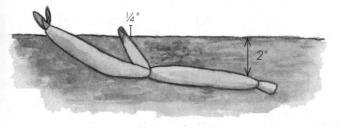

Plant the lotus rhizome so it is horizontal with sprouts pointing upward at a slight angle and the end opposite the section with the sprouts slanting slightly downward.

How to Harvest

The lotus has a long harvest season. It bears buds, flowers, and seedpods all at the same time, and all of these are edible, allowing it to be put to many uses simultaneously. Gather whatever part you want, as soon as it's ready.

For roots. Harvest the roots at the end of their growing season (usually September). Unless you have several plants, take just the last segment and store the rest of the root for planting next spring. If you've let your root grow to its full 4 feet, you can take several segments, either to plant or to eat. If you break them apart before storing, you'll find shoots growing from each segment by the time you come to plant them in the spring (assuming they've been stored properly).

Winter Storage

In many parts of the United States, you can overwinter lotus right in the water garden. Lotus are not as delicate as they look; they're hardy in many areas if they remain below the ice line. In a pond that freezes over but doesn't freeze solid, lower lotus containers to the bottom of the pond.

In Zones 5 or colder, move containers to a spot where they won't freeze solid or lift the plants to store over the winter. This is a very simple procedure. The lotus will go dormant as cold weather approaches. Remove the rhizome from its container and bury it in a container of damp sand (a bucket or a carton lined with plastic). Keep this container where it won't freeze but will stay cool enough to remain dormant and prevent it from starting to grow again; it needs its rest. Check every so often to be sure the soil has not dried out.

Varieties

Lotus is available from water-garden suppliers. Specify that you want the edible Chinese lotus. So far as I've been able to discover, all three of the lotus species described in this section are edible. Even our native American lotus (*Nelumbo lutea*) is edible; it was known and used by the Native Americans. Several varieties of Chinese lotus are available with flowers in shades of pink, yellow, and white.

All parts of the Chinese lotus are edible and can be eaten raw or cooked.

LEAVES. The young leaves can be added to a salad (gather only a few from each shoot). Or simmer briefly, toss with Asian sesame oil, and serve as a green vegetable.

PETALS. Float the petals in clear consommé or cold fruit soup, or use as a garnish for salads. You can dry the petals to enjoy them out of season.

SEEDS. The seeds can be dried and eaten out of hand like sunflower seeds or, in traditional Japanese fashion, pickled. Pickled lotus seeds are a classic ingredient in stir-fry dishes.

ROOTS. The root is by far the most widely used part of the vegetable. It's easily recognizable in any dish because slicing reveals the characteristic pattern of the air channels. Even when dipped in batter and fried as tempura, the pattern is clearly visible. Once you have acquainted yourself with the flavor, you'll think of many ways to use lotus root. I predict it will soon be as popular in your kitchen as in an Asian one. Other uses for the root are:

- Combine lotus root with shrimp, snow peas, and mushrooms for a quick but elegant company dish.

- Try adding sliced lotus root the next time you make sweet and sour pork; the sauce is particularly compatible with this fascinating vegetable.

Arrowhead

CI GU, CHEE KOO

Sagittaria sagittifolia

(color photo, page xvi)

Arrowhead is a beautiful bog plant, native to temperate regions throughout the world. This Asian species is much more widely used in Japan but also has its place in Chinese cuisine. It is also known by the names Chinese arrowhead, swamp potato, and kuwai.

Arrowhead is so pretty that it's grown in this country primarily as an ornamental. Once you've eaten it, however, you'll want to grow it as a vegetable as well.

Appearance

The graceful 10-inch-long leaves of this plant are shaped like giant arrowheads, hence the name. The lovely, three-petaled white flowers with pronounced golden yellow centers grow on long stems that stand out among the dark-green foliage; tubers are gray or yellowish gray.

How to Grow

Getting started. Arrowhead is a rampant grower. You have to repot it every year or it will become potbound after the first season. If you use a great many of the tubers in the kitchen, make a point of setting some aside for next year's crop.

Planting. Since arrowhead is a bog plant, set it no more than 3 to 6 inches below the surface of the water. Plant sparsely, to allow room for the growth of the roots, one plant to a 7-inch-diameter, 5-inch-deep pot; six plants to a 19-inch-diameter, 9-inch-deep pot.

How to Harvest

You can harvest arrowhead all season long, without any need to store it.

Winter Storage

If your water garden is large enough that the water doesn't freeze solid and the mud doesn't freeze, you can successfully overwinter arrowhead. The Asian species is somewhat less hardy than the American (hardy to Zone 5).

Varieties

The American arrowheads *Sagittaria latifolia* and S. *cuneata* closely resemble the Asian species. Their tubers, also called wapato and duck potato, can be used interchangeably with the Asian species. Lewis and Clark describe arrowhead as "a principal article of traffic" among the Native Americans they encountered. The women waded into the water to free the tubers from the pond bottom and the men waited in canoes to gather the tubers that floated to the surface.

– CULINARY USES –

Only the roots (tubers) of the arrowhead plant are eaten. They are bitter when raw but develop a wonderful flavor when cooked. The flesh is cream-colored and similar in flavor to a very delicate, slightly nutty sweet potato. The American arrowhead is somewhat nuttier in flavor than the Asian species but not so much so that it will affect the authenticity of your Chinese dishes. Arrowhead tubers can be roasted like a potato or boiled.

BOILED ROOT. When boiled, arrowhead tubers can be used in many recipes. A simple way to prepare it is to boil until tender, slice thin, and serve with butter or Asian sesame oil. If any is left over, serve cold with a vinaigrette dressing.

PART TWO

GROWING CHINESE VEGETABLES

In the gardener's world, soil, sun, and water are essential elements: soil to provide nutrients, sun to aid the plants in converting nutrients into food for the plants, water to make the nutrients available. Nature manages to maintain a delicate balance in a seemingly casual, almost offhand way; gardeners can't be quite so casual when they manipulate nature to grow a vegetable garden.

One of the most important things to learn is that lack of success with a vegetable doesn't mean the gardener is a failure. Some seasons, growers do everything right and are still defeated by a sudden hailstorm, a drought, or a spell of unreasonable temperature. All gardeners must be philosophers and take the bad with the good. Fortunately, even in the worst season, the home gardener will always have some unexpected successes.

In the wild only the strongest, most rugged plants survive; in the vegetable garden, the most precious crop is sometimes a comparatively delicate plant that must be coddled. Vegetable gardeners can take a tip from nature: The healthiest plants are the ones that produce the most and the tastiest crops, and they're the most resistant to disease and the vagaries of the weather. But how to produce this ideal crop? In this part of the book, we'll look first at how to succeed on a small scale, by planting your Chinese vegetables in containers, and conclude with what should actually be the first item on your list when you're creating a garden: how to improve your soil.

8

CHINESE CONTAINER GARDENS

If you're particularly proud of the philodendron in your office that has climbed over the door and is rapidly heading for the other wall, visualize instead a Chinese cucumber vine rampant all over your window. The vine, and its fresh crisp fruit, will astonish your coworkers.

Container gardening is something you can enjoy on a city windowsill, a balcony, or a country patio. Container gardening with Chinese vegetables is even more practical, easier, and more fun than growing ordinary vegetables. Even if you garden in the ground, you may want to start seeds indoors in containers to get a jump on the growing season.

Chinese vegetables make ideal container plants. The pots on this deck hold snow peas (A), Asian cucumbers (B), Chinese broccoli (C), garlic chives (D), asparagus peas (E), mizuna (F), and cilantro (G).

171

Why Garden in Containers?

Container gardening is very different from in-the-ground gardening. No roto-tilling, tiptoeing through muddy soil, or devising traps for rabbits. The space between rows of plants is never compacted by being walked on, weeds are almost nonexistent, and many pests are eliminated. It's much less effort, and your plants are right within view — a feast for the eyes as well as the palate. Also, and not to be minimized, there are the conversational advantages: you'll amaze your friends.

Another advantage is that your mistakes are never obvious. If a plant fails, its container can be temporarily retired to a screened corner with your other garden supplies, with no one the wiser. Only your best efforts need be on display. This is good for the gardener's morale! As it happens, container gardening is less prone to many of the plagues of the in-the-ground garden, so you probably won't lose your crop to slugs or cutworms.

Choosing a Site

The most obvious places for container gardens are windowsills, balconies, patios, and rooftops. Sunrooms are wonderful, if you have one. Front steps are also fairly obvious, and you can even put containers on your lawn. When you've exhausted those possibilities, look around again.

Vertical space. After the ground-level sites, there's still the air. Hanging containers are both suitable and attractive for many Chinese vegetables. Cucumbers don't care whether they grow up or down, neither do snow peas and yard-long beans. Arrange rows of baskets up and down a wall or trellis. Rig a metal pole horizontally across an open space to hold a number of hanging plants. Use stepladders or concrete blocks to increase your space vertically without crowding plants.

If you don't have a fence or balcony, many Chinese vegetables will grow up a single pole firmly planted in a pot. (Place a few small rocks in the pot before you add soil to add weight and stability.) This is pretty and practical; harvesting is easy and you won't miss any of the crop. Herbs can be planted around the base of the pole.

Custom shelving. For winter gardening indoors, build shelves across a window to triple your windowsill space. Take advantage of planters that combine shelves and fluorescent lights. A large one in front of a living-room window will yield fresh vegetables all winter. Or put fluorescent lights under the cabinets over your kitchen counter and grow your own herbs.

Greenhouses. Though it's a little expensive, a window greenhouse is a tremendous help where space is limited. It takes the place of your window and projects out from the side of the building. It will hold a surprisingly large number of plants. If, in addition, you build your windowsill out into the room by extending it with a shelf, or placing a table next to it, you can have a sizable area. This increases your growing season at both ends (spring and fall) and allows you to get an early start without taking over every available surface within your apartment.

Greenhouses are even more expensive but offer even more space. They come in every size, starting with small units that hold only a few trays and sit up against the house. That's a subject for a whole different book, though.

Choosing Your Containers

You can't pick your container unless you know what it is to hold, but on the other hand, you can't plan what to put in your container until you know what you want to grow and how much room it requires. (For plant requirements, see the container vegetables guide starting on page 180.)

You can grow plants in anything that will hold a soil mixture and drain excess water (which usually means punching a few holes in strategic places). Aesthetics aside, a container can be many of the things you usually throw away — large yogurt or cottage cheese containers, milk jugs with the tops cut off, egg cartons (for seedlings), wooden crates, 5-gallon buckets, and much, much more. Many items discarded because they no longer perform their original function make ideal containers. A chipped rim may spoil a piece of pottery, but not if it's completely covered by foliage. Yard sales are a great place to pick up odd plates for putting underneath pots, as well as baskets and other decorative vessels to use as disguises for recycled yogurt containers.

Ceramic containers. You can have a more conventional garden with classic clay pots; these are available in a variety of sizes and range from plain to elaborate and expensive. Check the decorative types for drainage holes. You can often drill holes in pottery with a high-speed drill, but there's always a risk of cracking. If you don't want to risk a favorite piece, use it to hold a smaller pot with good drainage.

Plastic pots. These are the easiest option. Plastic is cheap, easy to clean, readily available, and lightweight. Weight is especially important for large containers, and for rooftop gardens or balconies. Plastic pots come in all sizes and colors, though you may have to hunt around to find the style you want. If you're willing to spend more money, you can buy plastic pots or other synthetic materials designed to look like terra-cotta, as well as ornamental planters for more formal situations.

Large-scale pots. For really large containers, plastic whiskey barrels are a good choice. These are much lighter than wood half-barrels, though you may prefer the look of wood. With a couple of rocks in the bottom, plastic tubs are just as good as the wooden ones for support that offsets the bushiest, tallest, most heavily fruited plant. They fit in equally well with kitchen cast-offs and elegant Chinese porcelain.

A close second, in my opinion, are the old galvanized-iron washtubs, which have the advantage of convenient side handles and a surface that lends itself to either the simplest or the most elaborate artistic treatment. Just use a spray can for an occasional change of color or elaborate decoration. For drainage, simply pry the bottom loose of its rim in four places and cover these openings with gravel.

Under-pot protection. Containers need some sort of saucer or tray underneath to catch water. On a windowsill or table this is obvious, less so for outdoor container gardens. A great option for a windowsill is a single tray that runs the width of the window, which allows you to crowd plants closer together than individual saucers permit. A saucer reduces your watering chores by holding water (and liquid fertilizer) long enough for plants to absorb it. On the other hand, few plants besides watercress tolerate sitting in water for more than a couple hours. During rainy spells you must dump out the water in outdoor trays to keep plants from rotting.

For really large containers, trays are impractical. Fortunately, since these hold more soil and therefore more water, a tray is less important. Unless you're gardening on a wooden deck, large containers can sit right on the paving. Self-watering containers don't need a tray; these are now available in all sizes. If you want the option of moving large containers, place them on a wheeled caddy. These handy items are either wood or metal and are available at garden centers.

Containers on a wooden deck can cause boards to rot. Placing pots on trays or saucers helps prevent this, especially if elevated on a couple of narrow scraps of wood to allow the boards underneath to dry. Even better are the terra-cotta pot "feet" sold at many garden suppliers. These do great job of preventing rot for pots with or without a tray. Or look for a planter with built-in feet.

Getting the Light Right

Vegetables require sun, or its equivalent in light. Six to eight hours of direct sun is the most a plant needs for fruit production (cucumbers, eggplants, hot peppers). Foliage vegetables and root crops produce with only four hours of sun. Some foliage vegetables settle for a bright north or east window; some herbs, such as watercress, grow well with surprisingly low light levels.

If your problem is not enough sun, get creative. On a terrace or rooftop, paint the wall behind the plant white to get more mileage out of existing sun. Mulch with aluminum foil; this helps preserve moisture and repel aphids while increasing the amount of light. Try fashioning a sun reflector: Staple foil on a frame of a suitable size, stand it to face the sun, and reflect it onto the plant. To get maximum benefit from this device, move it as the sun moves. Remember to take it away if the weather turns very hot.

Temperature control. Don't confuse light with heat. Cool-weather crops, such as Chinese broccoli and snow peas, like sun but not heat. If you grow them on a rooftop or terrace, the surface on which they stand may get very hot. After a couple of weeks of very hot, dry, and possibly windy weather, your plants will begin to look stressed. Protect them either by moving them to partial shade or by creating partial shade over them. Plant caddies with casters make it easy to move even big containers. If moving is impractical, cover with a row cover. Or construct movable lath walls tall enough to create partial shade for part of the day. Build them with horizontal wooden bases designed to keep the walls from blowing over.

Indoor lighting. Plants in a sunny windowsill can get too much sun and heat at certain times of the year. That's easy to control with gauzy curtains that you draw when the sun is strongest and brightest (which isn't necessarily high noon), then open so the plant gets the maximum number of sun hours.

In the winter, or in windows that don't get full sun, use fluorescent tubes to supplement available light. Vegetables that set fruit usually won't produce under fluorescent light alone. If you want a plant to set fruit, you must provide sunlight plus enough supplemental light to make up whatever hours are lacking. In the short winter days of northern regions, even a window with good sun exposure may not be enough. Ordinary fluorescent bulbs are good enough for starting seedlings or growing leaf crops, but for eggplants and peppers you'll need the wide-spectrum bulbs (grow-lights) available from garden suppliers.

Garden-supply catalogs offer fixtures designed to reflect maximum light and pulleys that make it easy to raise and lower fixtures. Any fluorescent light fixture should be movable. For a large fixture, the simplest method is to hang it from the ceiling by a chain that can be raised and lowered by its links. You'll need to raise and lower lights to accommodate different-sized plants. For starting seedlings, lights need to be just a couple of inches above the seedlings, and the lights have to go higher as the seedlings grow higher. If you're keeping peppers coming on a mature plant, the light has to be much higher to clear the top of the plant.

Seedlings are very sensitive to low light levels and quickly get tall and spindly as they reach for better light. Don't let that happen or the plants will always be weak. Adequate light is just as important to immature as to mature plants; it's not an ingredient you can skimp on. (See page 201 for more about starting seedlings.)

Invest in a timer. Set it to turn the lights off and on automatically, adjusting the schedule as needed.

Soil for Containers

As with any type of gardening, soil is critical. Avoid bringing in baskets of earth from your yard. Garden soil is heavy, and watering makes it even heavier. This is a factor if you're gardening on a rooftop or in an apartment. The combined weight of your containers might be more than the roof can bear. In addition, garden soil in pots becomes too compacted. Another disadvantage is that it's not sterilized; garden soil can bring outdoor pests and diseases inside.

For container gardening, use a soil-less growing mix, usually a blend of peat moss and vermiculite, and sometimes perlite. You can buy these in small or large quantities at any garden center, or you can make your own. Many commercial mixes contain fertilizer as well.

MAKING YOUR OWN SOILLESS POTTING MIX

Most soilless mixes are composed — more or less — of equal parts of peat moss and vermiculite, plus fertilizer. Always moisten your soil mix before using. You may need to let it sit for 15 minutes so it has time to absorb water. Some commercial mixes contain a wetting agent to speed up the process (this helps the peat moss absorb water). If you purchase a small bag that feels reasonably heavy, it may be premoistened, but a large "bale" of potting mix is rarely premoistened.

MY FAVORITE LARGE-BATCH SOIL MIX

To mix this formula, I dump all the ingredients into a plastic garbage can, cover it, and roll it (on its side) back and forth, or over and over, until the contents are thoroughly blended. A glance inside the can tells me if everything is well mixed.

12 cubic feet of peat moss

12 cubic feet of vermiculite

5 pounds of a "complete" fertilizer (I use 5-10-5)

5 pounds of limestone (less for plants that like acidic soil)

2 pounds of rock phosphate

CORNELL UNIVERSITY SOILLESS MIX

If you don't need a large quantity, here's a smaller recipe. This is the original soilless mixture developed at Cornell University for container plants. I think it's easier to skip the dried manure and superphosphate and substitute time-release fertilizer, but don't add that when you make up this mix. Time-release fertilizers should be added just before potting.

8 quarts vermiculite

8 quarts shredded peat moss

8 tablespoons dried cow manure or steamed bonemeal

2 tablespoons ground dolomitic limestone

2 tablespoons superphosphate (0-20-0)

Keep your soilless mix in a covered container when not in use, so it stays sterile. Keep the tools you use for working with it as clean as possible also. (I keep a plastic scoop right in the container.) If you garden with things that go into the dishwasher (many people use kitchen spoons), you can be sure your utensils won't spread disease from one container to another.

Fertilizer for Containers

Any good garden fertilizer works for containers, but some types are particularly handy. (See page 196 for more about fertilizers.) Any formula that's described as being good for vegetables will give you a satisfactory crop, and you won't have to do anything except follow the recommendations on the label. With outdoor container gardens, remember that rainfall is constantly washing out nutrients, so these need fertilizing more often than plants growing inside or in the ground. This is especially true after a long rainy stretch. (In dry weather, when you're supplying all the plants' water, this is less of a problem.) Indoors or out, it's safest to feed frequently but lightly.

Time-release fertilizers. These are a boon for today's busy gardeners because they're added once and last all season. Mix into the soil before potting (the label usually gives amounts for pots of different sizes). That may be all you need, but keep an eye on your plants. Large vines and heavy-bearing plants may need a snack later in the season.

Liquid fertilizers. These make it easy to supply a late-season snack. Or you can use them all season long, feeding as you water. For container plants, dilute liquid fertilizer to at least half the strength recommended on the label. Some gardeners prefer to feed plants with quarter-strength fertilizer every couple of weeks.

Watering Containers

Watering outdoor containers isn't much different from watering an in-ground garden. Theoretically, plants need an inch of rain a week, but various conditions affect this. Some plants are thirstier than others. Large plants, and those with a big root system, need more frequent watering. A windy or very hot, dry day evaporates water much more quickly than a still or humid one.

You can set a small dish out near the plants; if the cat doesn't drink it, it will give you a rough record of rainfall. You can also buy a rain gauge, but I'd rather go by the appearance of each individual plant. Check the soil in each container. If it seems dry an inch down, it needs water. Don't let excess water stand in a saucer more than a couple of hours; most vegetables dislike having "wet feet" just as humans do.

If you've filled your containers properly, there will be an inch or two of space between the top of the soil and the rim of the container. Fill this space with water, then come back and do it again — three times in all. If you don't like watering, consider rigging up a drip irrigation system. You can put these on a timer for a fully automated system, but you still need to check plants because water needs change with the weather and as plants mature.

Watering hanging baskets. These have to be watered much more often than other containers. It's customary to line a hanging basket with sphagnum moss, but this dries out instantly. Line the basket with several layers of clear plastic, then line with *wet* (not damp) moss and fill with soilless mix. After the basket is filled, punch several drainage holes in the plastic with a knife or knitting needle. (With hanging pots, make holes in the plastic to conform to your container's drainage holes.) As long as you don't let the sphagnum moss dry out (and you can tell by the color of it through the plastic), your plant will always have a chance of making it. It is better not to let the mix itself dry out too much either, but the moss gives you a margin.

NOT FOR CONTAINER GARDENS

I would never say unequivocally that a vegetable can't be grown in a container; gardeners are ingenious and some seem to be able to grow anything they set their hearts on. There are some vegetables, however, that I feel are too much trouble or take up too much space in proportion to the crop they provide. I can't recommend them for container gardening, indoors or out.

I advise against winter melon because of its size; pickling melon and fuzzy gourd because of their limited use; fava beans; and soybeans. Some container gardeners do grow soybeans, and it certainly can be done successfully; I just give so many other vegetables a higher priority in my kitchen.

Container Vegetables, Plant by Plant

Since all of these vegetables are described in detail in other chapters, this section highlights only the special things you need to know in order to grow them successfully in containers. The areas not covered under general gardening (size of container and ability to grow indoors or under lights) are dealt with here. The vegetables are ordered alphabetically by botanic name. Chapter 7 gives container advice for water garden plants.

Bunching Onion, page 114
Allium fistulosum

No Chinese cook worth her soy sauce would consider going into business without a good supply of fresh bunching onions. These are easy to grow anywhere, so anyone can always have a container full. Indoors, grow bunching onions in a sunny window. They also do well under lights without supplementary sun. Dig up a plant from outdoors and pull off a clump, or start from seeds.

Use a pot at least 6 inches deep (8 inches is even better) and at least 8 inches in diameter. You can keep the clump within this diameter by harvesting the outside scallions; a wider pot accommodates a larger clump.

Water sufficiently to reach the roots. Keep the soil on the moist rather than the dry side, but not soggy. Feed monthly with diluted liquid fertilizer.

Garlic, page 117
Allium sativum

Since each clove grows into a bulb containing several cloves, garlic is a practical container and windowsill plant. You can start a second planting three to four months before you harvest your first crop. With careful planning, even the smallest kitchen need never run out of fresh, home-grown garlic.

Plant the cloves 1½ inches deep (2 inches in cold climates). Indoors you can do this any time of year; outdoors, plant in late fall. Garlic is truly winter hardy, so you don't have to take it indoors if you don't want to. An empty half whiskey barrel turned upside down, plus a straw mulch or a plastic covering over the whole container usually keeps garlic alive even in colder regions.

Put your garlic containers in full sun, whether on windowsill or terrace, and fertilize frequently with diluted fertilizer. Water frequently; don't allow the soil surrounding the roots to dry out completely. On the other hand, never let the containers stand in water or the bulbs may rot.

Garlic Chives, page 120
Allium tuberosum

A perfect plant for the indoor or outdoor container herb garden, garlic chives are not only delicious but also offer attractive flowers. The flowering extends over a long period. Even in my outdoor garden where wind, rain, and summer sun hasten the fading of flowers, garlic chives bloom profusely for months. You can clip the leaves and still get flowers, as long as you don't accidentally clip the flower stalks or take so much foliage you discourage bud formation.

Start in individual 4-inch pots. After several months your clump will be large enough to divide. Tuck a division into a larger container of other herbs or vegetables. Don't eat the bulbs, just the foliage (as with common chives), and always leave enough for the plant to grow on.

Pot some up to enjoy indoors over the winter; grow it on a sunny windowsill. It makes a pretty table centerpiece; try three or four pots in a Chinese basket to accent a Chinese meal. The fragrant white-flowered species (*Allium ramosum*) is particularly nice indoors.

Start seeds indoors anytime. Outdoors, early spring is best. The seeds are small and should be sown ½ inch to ¾ inch deep. If your sunny spots are preempted, garlic chives tolerate partial shade.

 ## Burdock, page 90
Arctium lappa

Burdock needs a container at least 12 inches deep — and practically nothing else. Since you're growing it in 12 inches of soil, you won't get a full 24-inch root. Just to be sure to harvest the roots as soon as they fill their container; they will be sweet and delicate. We eat baby carrots and baby beets, so why not baby burdock?

If you want, you can plant it outdoors in the fall and let it come up and surprise you in the spring. Indoors, you wouldn't want to tie up the room with such a hardy plant.

Germinate the seeds indoors; unlike the plant, the seeds like it warm and cozy. Soak overnight in warm water and plant the next morning 1 inch deep and 2 inches apart; thin to 4 inches apart.

 ## Mustard Greens, page 11
Brassica juncea

Chinese mustard makes an attractive container plant. The leaves of some varieties are deeply cut, others are beautifully curled, and red-stemmed varieties are colorful. Grow several varieties together, or group several plants flower pots, each with a different variety, for a pretty windowsill or terrace.

Chinese mustard doesn't take up much room. You can grow a single plant in a 4-inch pot. They combine well in a container with vegetables like beets or radishes, as well as with herbs of all kinds. Or plant a "mess" of greens — spinach, Swiss chard, and so on, all together.

You can grow them indoors under lights all winter; they will do very well, especially in a cool room. One thing that won't work is growing them on a city rooftop in midsummer without shade; they don't like heat.

Sow seeds ½ inch deep and about 2 inches apart. Thin and eat every other one. If you need just a few leaves to spike a salad, take the outer ones. Harvest whole plants by cutting them about three-quarters of the way down; each plant will send up new leaves (especially if you give it some fertilizer).

Mizuna, page 14
Brassica napa nipposinica

Because it grows quickly and can be harvested at any stage (like lettuce), mizuna is a particularly good vegetable for the container garden. It has beautiful light green foliage, distinctive and attractive. It will grow back after cutting or can be cropped a few leaves at a time. A few crops can be grown in one season, or it can make way for another vegetable.

Or grow mizuna indoors all winter. While it grows well in full winter sun, it doesn't require it and will thrive under lights or in a partly sunny window. In the summer, it may (again like lettuce) do better in partial shade, although it will only wilt, not bolt, if it gets too hot. Grow this exactly like Chinese mustard.

Flowering Kale, page 78
Brassica oleracea Acephala Group

If ever there was a natural for container gardening, it is flowering kale. The plant is compact, easy to grow, beautifully colorful, and deliciously edible. As if all that weren't enough, it even comes in miniature varieties to accommodate any container situation.

I like flowering kale best when grown alone, one to a container. Nevertheless, it is an excellent bedding plant and combines well with other vegetables or flowers. A 4-inch pot will hold one miniature variety, an 8-inch pot will hold one regular-sized plant.

You can grow flowering kale outdoors in the sun or indoors under lights. The miniature size is particularly attractive for indoors. The only difficulty with growing it indoors is that it needs cold weather to develop color. Until its foliage is "turned" by cold, it looks like a particularly lovely dark green cabbage with purple veins. If you grow it indoors, you may have to put it outdoors until the temperature has done its job.

Plant in midsummer for a fall crop. Start seeds in small flats for transplanting, or sow directly in the container where they are to grow. Cabbages grow on "stalks" that must be covered with soil, or else the weight of the head might break them. If you plant seeds directly into their permanent containers, leave space in the pot so you can add soil; it should come right up to the bottom of the mature cabbage head. Taking this into account, sow seeds ½ inch deep. Fertilize after a month.

The cabbages make the best eating when young, before they turn color. The colors are so beautiful that you may want to let them mature. As a compromise, eat the thinnings and leave one or more to develop color.

Chinese Broccoli, page 80
Brassica oleracea
Alboglabra Group

This is a good choice for container gardeners who want to grow broccoli; it takes up only half the space of common broccoli and is extremely prolific. It grows best outdoors or in a greenhouse.

Sow the seeds ½ inch deep and 1 inch apart in a 5-gallon container.

Thin young plants to stand 6 inches apart, and eat the thinnings. For a single plant, use a 12-inch pot. Keep plants evenly moist but not soggy. Feed when plants are six weeks old.

Pak Choy, page 83
Brassica rapa Chinensis Group

Pak choy is easy to grow and lends itself to container gardening, both indoors and out. Since it's leafy rather than fruiting, it does well under lights, which means you can enjoy it all winter.

Since it's a cool-weather vegetable, sow in early spring, or in midsummer for a fall crop. Indoors, you can sow it any time. You can harvest it like leaf lettuce, taking just the outside leaves until hot weather affects the growth. Or pick the whole spring crop, use the space for some other vegetable, then replant pak choy for fall or winter use. Quick-maturing vegetables like pak choy allow container gardeners to grow a greater variety of good things to eat.

Sow seeds ½ inch deep and 6 inches apart. Plant closer together and eat thinnings for an extra-early crop, or tuck a plant into a larger container with other vegetables such as radishes, garlic chives, and mizuna.

Keep well watered and fertilize every two or three weeks. Harvest it as needed, any time from five weeks on.

Chinese Cabbage, page 86
Brassica rapa Pekinensis Group

Since Chinese cabbage takes up less room than the common cabbage, you can grow it in a much smaller container. Ordinary cabbage needs 20 inches between plants, Chinese types need only 12; tall, slender varieties need even less. Use a 10- to 12-inch pot for the chunky napa types; an 8-inch pot will hold the more slender varieties. Sow seeds in place ½ inch deep in midsummer for fall eating. Thin to the recommended spacing for your particular variety.

Feed with half-strength fertilizer every couple of weeks and water copiously.

Cabbages grow best outdoors. Chinese mustards are a much better bet for indoor container gardens.

Hot Pepper, page 124
Capsicum frutescens

I don't know why "ornamental" peppers are such a popular house plant when the real thing is just as pretty and produces quantities of edible peppers. Hot peppers are ornamental at all stages of growth. The leaves are a glossy dark green, the white flowers with their yellow centers are delightful, and the peppers are colorful. The peppers go on being decorative if you dry them on strings to hang in the kitchen.

Sow seeds ¼ inch deep. Start your peppers in seed trays for transplanting or seed directly in 10- to 12-inch pots or larger containers. In a window box, space the plants about 18 inches apart. You can always prune them back if they get out of hand. In a large container, combine with greens and herbs for a handsome display. With flowers and fruits at the same time, peppers in outdoor containers stay decorative right through the summer. If a plant wears itself out, discard it and start a new one.

Indoors they grow all year-round. One plant indoors will surely be enough, especially since hot peppers require as much full sun as possible, and supplemental lighting won't do much for setting fruit if you skimp on direct sun.

Feed once a month, or use quarter-strength liquid fertilizer every week.

Garland Chrysanthemum, page 17
Chrysanthemum coronarium

Grow garland chrysnathemums (shun-giku) instead of common garden chrysanthemums, and you'll be able to have your flowers and eat them too. The combination of fragrance and flowers makes it a very attractive container vegetable. If you're willing to dispense with most of the flowers — the greens are, after all, the main crop — you can grow shungiku in a partially shaded spot, leaving your sunny areas for more demanding plants. On a rooftop, protect it from the wind. This will do well in a sunny window or under lights.

Plant in pots at least 4 inches in diameter in early spring. Larger pots give you larger plants. In a big pot, shungiku could grow to 4 feet, but if you harvest the leaves when the plant is 6 inches high it will never attain full growth. Harvesting or pinching off the top makes plants bushier rather than taller. The greens are ready to harvest in about 30 days. Shungiku is pretty combined with lettuces and other low-growing greens in a large, wide container.

Add fertilizer to your potting mix and fertilize again when seedlings are 3 inches high. Once the flowers form, the foliage turns bitter and isn't as good to eat. If you want shungiku to bloom, though, fertilize lightly when flowers form and every two weeks thereafter.

Cilantro, page 128
Coriandrum sativum

This makes an attractive addition to any container or windowsill and will also grow under lights. Tuck it in with other plants or grow it on its own. Cilantro doesn't like very hot weather; in midsummer, relegate it to a partly shady spot on a terrace and move it off a sunny windowsill. Or harvest the whole plant and start a new crop.

Sow seeds ½ inch deep in a pot that's 5 or 6 inches deep, or in a larger container with other vegetables or herbs. A container of lettuces and herbs is particularly nice because you have the makings for an instant salad all in one place. Cilantro bolts more quickly if transplanted, so it's best to plant seeds in the container they'll grow in.

As with all leafy crops, a nitrogen fertilizer is called for, but too much impairs flavor and invites insects. Feed with diluted liquid fertilizer every three weeks or so, as well as after harvesting a lot of leaves all at once.

Mitsuba, page 132
Cryptotaenia canadensis
ssp. *japonica*

Mitsuba (Japanese parsley) is grown primarily for its foliage, which looks very much like Italian parsley, only with a prettier leaf. It also forms a sturdier plant. It tolerates partial shade, so it does better on a windowsill in winter than parsley. It doesn't like a really hot, sunny spot; if you grow it on a sunny deck or patio, tuck it among taller plants to provide a little shade.

Plant anytime indoors, in very early spring outdoors. Sow seeds ½ inch deep, keep moist, and fertilize once a month.

Sweet Melon, page 29
Cucumis melo

Many Asian varieties of sweet melon weigh only 1 to 3 pounds and grow on shorter stems than cantaloupes and honeydews, so they're a better choice for containers. They are handsome growing up a rooftop or terrace wall.

Try growing them around chicken-wire cages. Start the plants *inside* the cage, then train the vines to grow around the outside; otherwise, you won't be able to get at the fruits. The vine doesn't climb by itself; you have to weave it through the cage or tie it to the wire with soft cord. Guide the flowers to the outside so the fruits form where you can reach them.

You can grow sweet melon indoors, if you're willing to give up a large sunny window for the 80 or 90 days they take to mature. The flavor of a freshly picked, vine-ripened melon is ambrosia compared to even the best melon you can buy in the store; it's well worth a try.

Like all melons, this is strictly a warm-weather crop. Sow seeds about four weeks after the last frost date in a 5-gallon container of soil mix enriched with plenty of fertilizer. Plant four seeds 1 inch deep and thin to two plants when the seedlings are 4 inches high. If you plant two different varieties in the same container, you can make it look like you have two kinds of melon growing on one vine. For an earlier crop, start the seeds indoors under lights.

Keep well watered at all times and fertilize every 20 days. Some melons may have to be supported with individual slings to keep them from slipping off their stems as they ripen.

Asian Cucumber, page 35
Cucumis sativus

A single vine grows well in a 1-gallon container, but I suggest using a 5-gallon container and planting several different varieties. They can comfortably intertwine on a trellis, and you'll have all different kinds growing together in one large cucumber "patch." Vines can be pinched back and trained to grow in any direction you please, including up or down. They'll even grow upside down from a hanging basket.

For an early crop, start indoors. Otherwise, sow the seeds ¾ inch deep and about 3 inches apart in your container. Thin to allow about 10 inches between plants when seedlings are 4 inches high.

Fertilize every three weeks. You must water copiously; cucumbers are as thirsty as melons, and that's saying a lot. The foliage will wilt in very hot weather, but that won't bother the plant a bit as long as the roots are moist and cool. If the foliage doesn't shade the base of the vine, mulch the surface of the container to help keep the roots happy. Remember, soil dries out much more quickly in a container than in an in-ground garden.

Chinese Pumpkin, page 40
Cucurbita maxima, C. moschata

For the container gardener who wants to grow pumpkins, which are too large for container culture, Chinese pumpkins are the perfect answer. Most varieties grow on short vines, and the fruits are small enough to be practical. They're also much more decorative and will climb a trellis or string; fruits can be supported by individual slings if any seem to be getting too heavy for the vine.

These require more space and sun than a winter window can provide. Try a different vegetable for inside unless you have a greenhouse to grow these.

The growing season is long, so start Chinese pumpkins indoors. Plant in 5-gallon containers — two plants per container — about four weeks after the last frost date. Plant two different varieties for a fascinating display.

Squash is a heavy feeder so fertilize weekly once the vines are 12 inches long. Frequent diluted feedings are best; overfertilizing makes plants brittle. Copious watering is necessary; the roots should never be allowed to dry out.

Daylily, page 94
Hemerocallis fulva

Daylilies are decorative in a container garden. They are best, however, grown outdoors. They grow well in sun or partial shade. Their straplike foliage and brilliant orange or yellow flowers provide the perfect background to low-growing plants.

The size of the container depends on the number of daylilies you wish to grow. To start with, choose a container twice the size of the clump. Daylilies spread rapidly, and you may find that they've soon outgrown their container. Overcrowding will mean fewer flowers, so divide clumps whenever they have outgrown their containers.

Since rain washes out nutrients, daylilies grown in containers benefit from very occasional feeding. If you repot each spring and mix in a little time-release fertilizer, you can forget about feeding until the following spring.

Luffa, page 44
Luffa acutangula

This is not a plant for indoors unless you have a bay window you want to turn into a jungle. On a terrace it would be spectacular, but you could grow a number of cucumbers or melons instead of one of these vines.

Sow seeds in a really large container (5 gallons minimum) three weeks after the last frost date. Plant 1 inch deep with three or four seeds to a container. Thin to one plant per container as soon as the third set of true leaves appears.

Keep the soil moist for the two or more weeks the seeds take to germinate. Protect the seeds and young seedlings if the nights turn chilly. This is strictly a warm-weather vegetable; if you need a sweater, so will luffa.

Fertilize weekly; this plant grows rampantly. Water copiously. Add a little lime from time to time because you constantly leach it out with watering, and the soil should be slightly alkaline.

don't require support. The reason for growing the vines up a support is to keep them from taking up all your garden space.

Sow seeds 1 inch deep in a really large container (5 gallons is the minimum size, larger is better). Fertilize when flowers appear, and again as the fruits form.

Start seeds indoors for an earlier crop, if you have space for the large container. Or sow outdoors in a protected spot as soon as all danger of frost is past. If you plant too early, cover the container with several layers to protect it from freezing temperatures.

Bitter Melon, page 48
Momordica charantia

Bitter melon is often grown purely as an ornamental and is worth a spotlight position since it is spectacular both in the flowering and in the fruiting stage. The copious watering it requires is much easier to provide in containers than in conventional in-the-ground gardens. In a container, you know that all the water is going to the melon roots, not into surrounding soil.

Bitter melon is a trellis plant, whether outdoors or in a greenhouse or sunroom, and requires full sun. The melons are small enough that they

Watercress, page 135
Nasturtium officinale

Watercress is a natural for the city apartment because it sits happily on almost any windowsill and prefers little or no direct sun. The most important requirement for growing watercress in a container is fresh water. Change the water once a day by emptying yesterday's water out of the dish and filling it with fresh water run through the top of the pot. You can start it from seeds but I never do; I use a fresh bunch from the market (see page 136). Add lime to the soil mix when rooting the plant, and monthly thereafter. Use a weak solution of liquid fertilizer every couple of weeks.

Harvesting won't hurt the plants a bit. In fact, you *must* pick it occasionally to keep the plants from getting too tall, or from going to seed.

 ## Snow Pea, page 98
Pisum sativum var. macrocarpon

When I tell container gardeners they can grow peas on their apartment windowsills, they look at me in disbelief. No sensible city gardener is going to give up valuable windowsill space for a handful of peas. If they give this amazing vegetable a chance, they're always delighted with the results. If you have a terrace wall, a balcony, or even some straight poles in a container, you can grow a sizable crop.

Snow peas are very prolific and produce with an abandon that makes a windowsill area seem like much more. Their beautiful lavender blossoms are as profuse as the pea crop.

Since snow peas require 8 to 10 inches of soil depth, you may need to set the container on the floor once plants have grown tall enough to reach the light. This is one crop that fruits under lights, but pick a dwarf variety. (This is probably your best bet for a windowsill, too.) Rigorous pinching back is necessary even with the dwarf varieties; otherwise the vines will soon be growing over the lights instead of under them. Dwarf varieties shouldn't require strings or other support, but they may do better and grow taller with something to grow on. Try them both ways and see what works for you.

Outdoors on a terrace, snow peas can be sown while you're still shivering from the cold, about six weeks before the last frost date in your area. Sow the seeds in a 4-inch-deep trench. When plants are about 6 inches high, fill in the trench with soil mix.

Keep the soil well watered; it should always feel a little damp to your fingertips. Side-dress lightly or water with diluted liquid fertilizer every two weeks.

 ## Asparagus Pea, page 102
Psophocarpus tetragonolobus

Asparagus pea is an excellent plant for container gardening: decorative, prolific, and easy to grow. The vines need strings, a pole, or a small trellis for support. If you don't want to bother with these or don't have much space, grow the other, much smaller species (*Lotus tetragonolobus*). It's small enough to fit in hanging baskets.

Asparagus pea requires full sun and prefers cooler temperatures than most houses are kept at. To grow it indoors over the winter, pick a room you keep on the cool side and set the pot or window box in the sunniest window. For best results, plant in a "ditch" so you can add soil to the container, and cover up the first few inches of the vine as it grows. Since it takes only 50 days to mature, you can sow it over and over again during the winter.

Outdoors, start it in early spring since plants are frost hardy and do best in cool weather. Sow seeds ½ inch deep and about 4 inches apart in a deep window box. Or sow 3 inches apart in a circle in a round 5-gallon container. Train each vine to a single string. Fertilize when the flowers first form.

Chinese Radish, page 105
Raphanus sativus

From the moment the first true leaves appear, Asian varieties look different from other radishes. Daikon, for one, offers beautiful gray-green, oddly cut leaves instead of the familiar coarse radish foliage. Other Chinese radishes come in all colors and sizes.

Chinese radishes can be grown outdoors, indoors, and under lights, all with equal facility. It's the easiest vegetable to grow and one of the quickest. Most varieties are sown in midsummer for fall and winter use. There are Chinese radishes for spring and summer too, just read your seed catalogs

carefully. Spring varieties are handy for intercropping with slower-growing vegetables; they're picked and gone long before your Chinese broccoli or eggplants need the space.

Sow smaller varieties 1 inch deep and 1 inch apart; larger varieties must be spaced proportionately. Thin out as they get crowded. Even tiny radishes make good eating, and the leaves of young radishes are as delicious as the roots. Fertilize lightly but often. Water regularly so that growth isn't checked by a dry spell.

Sesame, page 139
Sesamum indicum

Here's another Chinese herb that's so easy to grow and yet so ornamental that I can't imagine why more gardeners don't give it room as a houseplant. When someone expecting the usual collection of flowering house plants asks what this one is, the usual reaction to your answer is, "It's a *what?*"

Sow the seeds ½ inch deep in 3-inch pots. Transplant to moderately large containers with other herbs and vegetables, or to 6-inch pots for individual display. You won't know ahead of time what color flowers any given plant will produce, so it's fun to have several growing.

Sesame will take as much sun as you can give it. In containers, unlike in the open garden, it needs regular watering because there isn't anywhere else it can go for a drink.

Chinese Eggplant, page 110
Solanum melongena

This is a perfect vegetable for the container gardener, a showpiece both indoors or out. You can even grow it under lights; it's one of the few plants that fruits under those conditions.

Start the seeds indoors and don't move outside until the weather has warmed up. Transplant into 3-gallon containers, one per pot. Eggplants are heavy feeders. Once plants are outdoors, feed every couple of weeks with half-strength liquid fertilizer. Water copiously so roots never dry out; this means every few days in very hot, dry weather.

Adzuki Bean, page 62
Vigna angularis

Adzuki are bush beans and very similar to snap beans in their culture. They could easily replace common beans in the container garden. Adzukis bear prolifically (an important factor to the container gardener) on compact, attractive plants with numerous flowers in season. Several pots could be arranged to form a nice 2-foot-high hedge to edge a deck or patio.

The practical way to grow them is one plant to a container. The container should be 10 to 12 inches deep and at least 6 inches in diameter. Sow three seeds to a pot, and thin to one when the seedlings have their second set of true leaves. Adzuki beans grow better in a little acidity, so add a little peat moss to your soil mix (or less limestone, if you use my recipe). Fertilize when seedlings are about 4 inches high and every two weeks thereafter. Water regularly.

Mung Bean, page 65
Vigna radiate

Though mung beans are pole beans, and so take up more room than bush beans, they are still well suited to container gardening. They'll wrap themselves around anything handy. You'll have to train them to whatever support you provide — and keep them off your other vegetables.

Mung beans do best in really hot weather. Since they have a long growing season, set your containers in the warmest, least windy place you have. If you can, place the containers against a wall and rig up a sheet of plastic to lower over them during cool nights. Drop the plastic an hour or so before sundown; the cover will keep in the warmth built up in the wall during the sunny hours, and the beans will stay cozy all night.

If you can rig up this kind of protective plastic housing, you can plant the beans as soon as the days warm up; otherwise, wait until night temperatures reach 60° to 65°F. Plant the seeds 4 inches apart in a long, narrow container that's at least 14 inches deep. Fertilize when the pods start to form.

Mung beans can be grown indoors if you train them in front of a sunny window.

Yard-Long Bean, page 71
Vigna unguiculata ssp. *sesquipedalis*

Yard-long beans are great for the adventuresome container gardener. The vines aren't aggressive or over-long, the deep lavender flowers are large and beautiful, and the long, slender beans are fascinating and delicious to eat. The vines are so prolific you may have to pick them every day, like snow peas. Don't try them indoors unless you have a heated greenhouse.

The one factor that's critical to success is the temperature. Don't plant the seeds in outdoor containers until night temperatures are at least 65°F. You can start harvesting within 40 days, so there's no need to rush the planting.

Use containers at least 14 inches deep, as plants need 12 inches of soil. Sow seeds 1 inch deep and with 4 inches between seeds. Give each vine a pole to climb. Fertilize about once a month.

Ginger, page 144
Zingiber officinale

Even if the fresh root were not essential to Chinese and many other cuisines, ginger would be worth growing merely as an ornamental houseplant. Start with a whole knob showing at least one bud; plant it 3 inches deep in a 6-inch pot. When the shoots have reached about 10 inches, repot in a larger container. From then on, repot as needed. A 5-gallon container accommodates the full-sized plant. Fertilize every two weeks with half-strength liquid fertilizer.

Keep the soil moist. If you grow it in the house, put the pot on a tray of pebbles and keep the pebbles moist to humidify the air around the plant.

Don't put ginger in full sun until shoots are 3 inches high; partial or even full shade is better. It can be set outdoors once the air is warm and the nights no longer cold. Bring indoors for the winter when the nights drop down to around 50°F. (See page 146 for how to give plants a rest.)

9

WHERE IT ALL BEGINS: THE SOIL

Soil comes in two grades: topsoil, which is the first thing (you hope) that you encounter when you dig into the ground; and subsoil, which is the next layer of soil and is in the process of gradually turning into topsoil. This process can require over 200 years; obviously you should cherish your topsoil.

Growing cultivated flowers and vegetables depletes the nutrients in the topsoil. If these are not replaced, the soil becomes poorer and poorer, and less and less able to support vegetation. Fertilizer can replace some of the nutrients, but in order to prevent depletion, topsoil must also be restocked with organic matter

Organic Matter

The U.S. Department of Agriculture, in spite of a disposition to chemical fertilizers, reports: "Soils that have a high content of organic matter usually have many desirable physical properties. For example, they are easy to till, absorb rain readily, and tend to be drought-resistant. Because soils high in organic matter have these desirable properties, some people have speculated that they might also produce plants of superior nutritional quality and that the use of organic composts or manures would result in plants of superior quality to those produced with inorganic fertilizers." Subsequent studies have shown this to be the case; vegetables grown on organically fertilized soil are richer in essential vitamins and minerals.

Unlike fertilizer, *it is impossible to add too much organic matter to the soil.* This is why organic gardeners prize their compost heaps so highly. If you don't have room for a compost heap (Really? Not even an indoor earthworm bin?), not to worry. You can buy it by the bag, or by the truckload if you need more than you make. Mulching is another way to add organic matter.

Compost is the best source of organic matter, as well as being a not-very-concentrated fertilizer. If you make it yourself by recycling your own "garbage," it's absolutely free. Potato peelings, wilted lettuce, eggshells, coffee grounds, everything except meat and oils (but fish is good, and fish bones). This should all go into the soil, instead of into the garbage pail. Some city container gardeners put their vegetable leavings in the blender with a little water and add the resulting "soup" to the soil in their containers.

If you live near a stable or in a town like mine where there are horses or pet rabbits, you have another source of free fertilizer. Stable manure is a

GOOD SOURCES OF ORGANIC MATTER

- Alfalfa meal
- Compost
- Chopped leaves
- Grass clippings (if free of herbicides)

- Seaweed
- Manure (aged, composted, or dehydrated)
- Sawdust (mix with manure or other nitrogen source)

little messier, because it must be well rotted before it can be used on plants. You can, however, turn fresh manure into the soil in the fall and it will then be ready for spring planting. Rabbit manure can be dug in right around the plants, and it's amazing how much excellent fertilizer is produced by even one pet rabbit.

Soil Tests

You can't tell your soil's fertility merely by looking at it; you need a soil test. A soil test is simply a chemical analysis of the soil. You can do it yourself with a kit you buy at your local garden center, or you can send away to have it done. The Cooperative Extension Services used to do this, but now some refer you to private labs. (See the Appendix for soil-testing labs.) Send in the sample in late fall or early spring so that you have time to correct the soil balance before sowing your seeds.

The soil test tells you which nutrients are deficient in your soil. It also tells you if you need to adjust your soil's pH, and how to do this.

Acidic or Alkaline?

The acidity of your soil controls the availability of nutrients. If your soil's too acidic or too alkaline, all the fertilizer in the world won't help you grow good vegetables, because the nutrients will be locked up, unavailable to plants. You can tell whether your soil is too acidic or alkaline with a simple a pH-testing kit. These are included in most soil-test kits, or you can purchase one separately. A kit provides enough chemicals for several pH tests. For the most accurate results, send a soil sample to a lab for testing.

The pH reaction of the soil is measured on a scale that runs from 1 to 14. A measurement of 7 means neutral, neither acid nor alkaline. Numbers above 7 indicate alkaline, while numbers below 7 indicate acidity. Soils in various parts of the country have a natural tendency toward one or the other. In Connecticut, for instance, most soil was originally acidic. The Connecticut gardener can't count on this, though, because generations of farmers have worked to correct this acidity, plus areas on top of limestone outcrops may be naturally alkaline.

Most vegetables prefer a pH between 6.3 and 6.8, or slightly acidic, because that's the range of maximum nutrient availability. If soil contains ample organic matter to buffer pH, plants will tolerate a wider range. Snow peas and watercress prefer a slightly alkaline soil.

If a soil test shows your soil is too acidic (below 6.0) or too alkaline (above 7.5), the next step is to bring it to the desired pH. Always do so gradually, with several small applications rather than a single large one, or you'll end up with more of a problem than you started with. If your soil is too acidic, add ground limestone; follow the application rates on the label. Wood ashes can also be used to raise the soil pH.

If your soil is too alkaline, add sulfur along with organic material. Use acidic forms of organic matter, which include peat moss, ground bark, and sawdust. If you have access to pine needles, they make an excellent mulch.

Adding organic material every year helps correct either acidic or alkaline soils because it is an excellent buffer. In addition, it encourages the growth of soil bacteria and earthworms and decomposes into humus, which improves the texture of the soil and slowly fertilizes it as well.

Just What Is Fertilizer?

There's no coincidence that fertility and fertilizers are related. Fertilizers help you give back what plants remove from the soil, which you in turn remove when you harvest plants. There are three primary nutrients in most bags of fertilizer: nitrogen (N), phosphorus (P), and potassium (K). The numbers on the bags (for instance, 7-7-2 or 5-10-5) give the percentage, in NPK order, of these three nutrients that the mixture contains. Each element has its particular

function in plant growth, just as certain nutrients contribute to the health of certain parts of the human body (for instance, the calcium in milk builds bones while the iron in spinach contributes to the red blood cells).

Traditional, synthetic fertilizer blends tend to have higher analysis numbers such as 5-10-5 or 5-10-10. Organic fertilizer mixes tend to have lower numbers, but these don't tell the whole story. Synthetic blends often contain only N, P, and K and are designed to release these nutrients as quickly as possible. They may be called "balanced" or "complete" because they contain these three elements, but they don't contain all the essential nutrients. Because they are made from natural substances, organic fertilizers also contain micronutrients, which are also essential to plant growth.

I prefer organic fertilizers because they supply a wider range of nutrients and are less apt to harm plants or soil organisms. Synthetic fertilizers do not enrich the soil, nor do they nourish the soil bacteria or earthworms essential to the production of quality topsoil. Quite the contrary; high doses of concentrated synthetic fertilizers can harm soil organisms, and even more normal doses can stun them into ceasing their activity. Concentrated synthetics can burn plants (but then, so can chicken manure — even though it's organic, it's too concentrated). That's not to say that synthetic fertilizers aren't useful. When used in conjunction with abundant organic matter, and when used in moderation, synthetic fertilizers can produce good gardens.

Nitrogen

Nitrogen is the first element in a fertilizer formula (5-3-3, for example). The chief function of nitrogen is healthy leaf growth. In addition to iron, nitrogen is responsible for the dark-green color of foliage, and a lack of nitrogen may be indicated by pale-green or yellow leaves. (A lack of iron may have the same effect; as with the human body, the same symptom may result from more than one disease.)

Organic matter slowly releases nitrogen, thanks to the work of soil microorganisms. That's one of the reasons organic matter is so beneficial. But it's difficult to estimate how much nitrogen the soil organisms will release (it varies with temperature, among other things). Nitrogen is easily leached out by rain and watering, and it's used up in various natural soil processes. Vegetable plants use a lot of nitrogen, so soil tests almost always recommend applying this nutrient.

SOME COMMON ORGANIC SOURCES OF NUTRIENTS

Nutrient	Major Benefits	Sources	Signs of Deficiency
Nitrogen	Promotes growth of plant above ground, especially foliage	Dried or composted manure, fish emulsion, cottonseed meal, alfalfa meal/hay	Unnaturally pale green or yellow leaves
Phosphorus	Encourages strong stems and roots	Rock phosphate, fish emulsion, bone meal	Poor fruit set, plants grow slowly, dark or purple cast to foliage, yellowing of lower leaves
Potassium (Potash)	Increases winter hardiness, increases disease resistance, improves resistance to environmental stress, promotes root development	Greensand, granite dust, wood ashes	Lower leaves turn mottled and die, weak stems, leaf tips/edges look scorched or curl under

Nitrogen is not a difficult nutrient to obtain. If you don't use a blended fertilizer, you can buy large sacks of cottonseed meal, which is probably the least expensive source, or small, expensive sacks of dried blood. Fish emulsion and fish-and-seaweed fertilizers supply nitrogen. Rabbit manure is also high in nitrogen, so much so that some gardeners keep a pet rabbit just for the fertilizer it produces. Chicken manure contains so much nitrogen it can burn plants, so don't use it unless composted.

Too much nitrogen is harmful. It produces weak growth that invites insects, and it can give you all leaves with no melons or cucumbers. As long as you use organic fertilizers, or organic sources of nitrogen, it's unlikely that you'll apply too much; the soil bacteria must work on organic sources to convert it into a form the plant can utilize, and they usually maintain a good balance. If, on the other hand, you use synthetic fertilizers, it is possible to overdose. Synthetic forms of nitrogen are also easily washed away by rain (and if used in containers, by watering). If you use synthetic fertilizers, never exceed the recommended rates for application; it's safer to give smaller amounts more frequently.

Caution: After applying nitrogen sources, or fertilizer containing nitrogen, don't use lime or wood ashes for three or four weeks. You'll start a chemical reaction that causes nitrogen to evaporate. Conversely, don't spread fertilizer right after applying lime or wood ashes.

Phosphorus

The second number in a fertilizer formula stands for phosphorus. (Technically, it stands for the amount of phosphate, the most common form of phosphorus, but many gardeners erroneously use the terms interchangeably.)

Phosphorus makes everything else work in a plant's metabolism. In addition, it promotes strong stems and flowers, and aids in setting fruit. It is essential to root crops since it directly affects development of both feeder and main roots. If you get skinny roots instead of fat radishes, your soil is probably deficient in phosphorus.

Phosphorus is easy to apply and should always be included when side-dressing root vegetables. It's readily available in the form of rock phosphate, which is comparatively inexpensive. Additional sources are fish and shellfish. You don't have to bury fish heads in your garden, though; it's much easier to use fish emulsion. Some brands of fish emulsion are formulated to be higher in phosphorus (with a grade of 2-4-1, for example). Another source is bone meal.

Potassium

The last of the big three nutrients is potassium. Again, the number in the fertilizer grade technically stands for potash, a common form of potassium, but many gardeners use the terms interchangeably.

Its chief function is to promote healthy, sturdy plants that are more resistant to whatever stresses come along. It makes plants more winter hardy; it acts like the antifreeze in your car and so is particularly important to vegetables like garlic that overwinter in the ground.

A sufficient supply of potassium makes plants more resistant to diseases and less affected by extremes in temperature. It gives roots the strength to push deeply into the soil and is the most important of the three fertilizers for the production of satisfactory root crops.

Potassium is readily obtained if you have a source for wood ashes (which also add lime); they can be incorporated in the soil and used as a mulch. Be warned that in large quantities, wood ashes (as well as synthetic forms of potassium) can burn plant roots. Also, wood ashes raise soil pH so they may be helpful for acidic soils but should not be used on alkaline soils. Greensand and sulfate of potash-magnesia (langbeinite, sold as Sul-Po-Mag or K-Mag) are other organic sources that are readily available. Fish emulsion and fish-and-seaweed fertilizers also contain potassium.

Micronutrients

Other nutrients are essential but are needed in smaller amounts. These include calcium, magnesium, sulfur, and iron. A few more are needed in only trace amounts, so they're sometimes called trace elements: boron, copper, manganese, molybdenum, and zinc. The best way to ensure that your vegetable garden has enough of them is to use lots of compost or other sources of organic matter. All organic materials are good sources, as well as minerals including rock phosphate and granite dust.

Deficiencies of micronutrients are most often caused by soils being too acidic or too alkaline. This is especially true for iron. If your plants develop chlorosis (the classic symptom of iron deficiency in which leaves turn pale or yellow but veins remain deep green), it rarely means your soil lacks iron. It usually means the iron is locked up by soil that's too alkaline (as after overdosing with lime). Testing your soil's pH is the first step if you suspect a deficiency.

Oddly spotted or deformed leaves may indicate micronutrient deficiencies bad enough to interfere with your harvest. Try foliar feeding. Give your plants fish emulsion or fish-and-seaweed fertilizer, pouring it over plants so it wets the leaves. Plants can absorb nutrients more quickly through their leaves. That should help with this year's harvest. At the end of the season dig more organic matter into the soil to improve the overall supply and balance of micronutrients.

How to Fertilize

In general, follow the application rates on the package, as these will vary with each fertilizer. The easiest way to keep your vegetables well fed is to incorporate fertilizer into the soil at the beginning of the growing season and supply more as needed as plants grow. Use an all-purpose blend, or a fertilizer specifically formulated for vegetables (one such formula is 4-6-6). Mix it well with soil. Phosphorus, in particular, doesn't move through soil easily, so it's important to get it where roots can access it.

Most vegetables need supplemental feedings. You can scratch granulated fertilizer alongside plants, but it's easier to use a fish-and-seaweed fertilizer or fish emulsion. These are liquids, so you mix only a tablespoon or so per gallon of water, and you feed the plants as you water. Synthetic liquid fertilizers are also available. Some of these are concentrated, so to protect soil organisms, dilute to half or quarter strength and feed more often. As with any synthetic fertilizer, it works best in soils with abundant organic matter.

If you like to fine-tune things, feed leafy crops, such as amaranth, with a formula that's higher in nitrogen. Look for a product in which the first number is greater, such as 3-2-2. For rooting and fruiting vegetables, such as Chinese radishes and cucumbers, look for a formula in which the first number is lower, such as 2-4-1.

For container gardens, there's another option. Time-release fertilizers are engineered to release nutrients over a longer period, so they don't wash out as quickly. Theoretically, you can dig them into the soil at the beginning of the season and be done with fertilizing for the year. You may find that some plants need a snack as the season progresses, especially those that bear heavily or get cropped a lot. These fertilizers are more expensive, but if you have trouble remembering to fertilize, they're worth the extra money.

In the discussion of individual vegetables, I've given fertilizer recommendations. Don't take these recommendations as exact prescriptions. Variables of rainfall, soil, temperature, seeds, and many other factors affect how much fertilizer to apply and when. You can follow some general rules, but pay attention to the condition of your garden and the individual plants in it. You'll soon learn to distinguish between

Pests and Diseases

The healthier your plants, the more resistant they will be to pests and diseases. Aphids, whitefly, flea beetles, and powdery mildew will still make some inroads even on healthy plants. Many times insects can be sent packing with just a strong spray from the garden hose. As a last resort, the organic gardener can use insecticidal soap, pyrethrum, or rotenone.

Baking soda spray helps control some diseases such as powdery mildew. Try spraying plants with 4 teaspoons dissolved in a gallon of water (some people add 1 to 2 tablespoons of vegetable oil to help it stick). If you have trouble with a particular disease year after year, seek out varieties resistant to that disease.

Some insects, such as flea beetles, can be avoided by growing plants under floating row cover. For cucumbers and eggplants, you have to remove the row cover as soon as plants start to flower. Otherwise you'll keep out pollinating insects and will end up with no harvest.

A few insects here and there won't do much damage, so don't get nervous just because you see something walking around on a vegetable leaf. Remember that a vegetable garden is part of nature and you can't run it like a machine. Remember the old farmer who philosophically planted three cherry trees for every one he hoped to harvest. "One for the bugs, one for the birds, and one for me."

Starting Seeds Indoors

When you head to your local plant nursery or farmer's market in the spring, you probably won't find Chinese broccoli among the broccoli plants. If you want to get a jump on growing Chinese vegetables — in the ground or in containers — you need to start your own seeds indoors. It's easy, and it's fun to watch the little seedlings grow.

Containers and Planting Media

Use a soilless mixture, ideally one designed for starting seeds. (See page 177.) These are sterile, so your seedlings won't be flattened by the disease known as *damping off*. For the same reason, make sure your containers and any tools that come in contact with the potting soil are clean. At a minimum, wash in hot soapy water. If you've ever had a problem with damping off, sterilize your tools and containers in the dishwasher or with a 10 percent solution of bleach.

Some gardeners prefer to start seeds in individual small pots, soil blocks, or a tray of small cells. Others prefer to plant rows of seeds in small or large trays. For many vegetables it doesn't matter, but for the cucurbits and other large or fast-growing plants, the individual pots are a good idea. If you start these in individual peat pots, you can plant the whole pot in the ground and minimize transplanting shock.

Temperature and Light

Most seeds germinate best when it's warm, so put pots or trays in a warm spot until they sprout. If you start seeds is an unheated garage or basement, purchase a heat mat to speed things up.

Seedlings need more intense light than full-grown plants to ensure sturdy, stocky growth. In the short winter days of northern regions, a windowsill probably doesn't supply enough. Unless you have a greenhouse, grow seedlings under fluorescent lights with an automated timer set so lights are on 16 hours a day. (In cooler locations, seedlings should do reasonably well with 12 to 14 hours of light.) The lights should be just a few inches above plants; you'll need to keep raising them as plants grow. Or prop your seedlings on boards or cartons and remove these as plants grow.

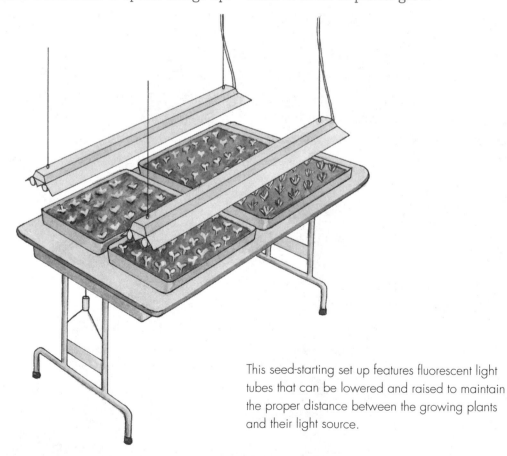

This seed-starting set up features fluorescent light tubes that can be lowered and raised to maintain the proper distance between the growing plants and their light source.

Thin seedlings with scissors
to avoid distrubing the roots
of adjacent plants.

When "True" Leaves Appear

Whatever container you start seeds in, thin plants (cut with scissors) or transplant to individual or larger containers as soon as the plants have a set of true leaves. (True leaves are small look-alikes of the plant's mature leaves; ignore the first set of small leaves, known as "seed leaves," that develop.) Ideally, seedlings should be far enough apart that leaves are just touching. If roots start growing out the bottom, plants need a larger container.

Fertilizing Young Seedlings

If your seed-starting mix doesn't include fertilizer, start feeding plants once they have their second set of true leaves. Feed weekly with half-strength fish-and-seaweed fertilizer, or a standard liquid fertilizer diluted to one-quarter strength.

Preparing for Life Outdoors

Seedlings need to be acclimated to the outdoors before you set them out. Do this gradually over two weeks. Start putting them outside for a couple of hours in the morning or late afternoon. After a few days increase the time to three hours, then four hours, up to a full day.

When you transplant seedlings into the ground, do it late in the day. Or shade plants under row cover or an upside-down carton to minimize transplant shock. Water plants well to settle the soil around their roots.

APPENDIX

Botanical, English, and Chinese Names

Mandarin Chinese pronunciation guide: c = ts (as in cos**ts**); q = ch (as in **ch**ew); x = sh (as in **sh**oe); z = ds (as in bir**ds**); zh = j (as in **j**ump)

Botanical Name	Common English Name	Mandarin Name	Cantonese Name	Alternate Common Names
Allium ampeloprasum	elephant garlic	da tou suan	dai suen tou	giant garlic
Allium fistulosum	bunching onion	cong	chin choong	Welsh onion, Japanese leek, nebuka, scallion, spring onion, multiplier onion, green onion
Allium sativum	garlic	suan	suen tou	
Allium tuberosum	garlic chives	jiu cai	gow choy	Chinese chives, Chinese leek, nira
Amaranthus hypo-chondriacus (seeds)	vegetable amaranth			
Amaranthus tricolor (leaf)	vegetable amaranth	xian cai	een choy	Chinese spinach, edible amaranth, hiyu, callaloo, bhaji
Arctium lappa	burdock	ngao pong	niu pang	gobo, edible burdock
Benincasa hispida	winter melon	dong gua	tung kwa	white gourd, wax gourd, ash melon, calabaza China
Benincasa hispida var. *chieh-gua*	fuzzy gourd	mao gua	tsit gua	hairy melon, hairy gourd, hairy cucumber
Brassica juncea	mustard greens	jie cai	gai choy	Indian mustard, takana, Chinese mustard
Brassica napa nipposinica	mizuna	ri ben shue cai		Chinese potherb mustard, Japanese salad green, ri ben, shue cai
Brassica oleracea Acephala Group	flowering kale	wu tou gan lan	hwa choy	ornamental kale, flowering cabbage

Botanical Name	Common English Name	Mandarin Name	Cantonese Name	Alternate Common Names
Brassica oleracea Alboglabra Group	Chinese broccoli	jie lan	gai lan	Chinese kale, white flowering broccoli
Brassica rapa Chinensis Group	pak choy/choi	bai cai	bok choy	Chinese or white mustard cabbage
Brassica rapa Pekinensis Group	Chinese cabbage	huan ya bai	wong nga pak	napa cabbage, hakusai, Tianjin cabbage, michihili, Chinese celery cabbage
Capsicum frutescens	hot pepper	la jiao	lat jiao	chili pepper
Chrysanthemum coronarium	garland chrysanthemum	tong hao cai	tong ho	edible chrysanthemum, shungiku
Colocasia esculenta 'Fontanesii'	violet-stemmed taro	yu tou	woo chai	black taro, black elephant ear
Coriandrum sativum	cilantro	xian choy	yan sui	coriander, Chinese parsley
Cryptotaenia canadensis ssp. *japonica*	mitsuba	san ye	san ip	Japanese parsley
Cucumis melo	sweet melon	xiang gua	tian gua	Asian melon, Oriental melon
Cucumis melo Conomon Group	pickling melon	yue gua	uet kwa	uri
Cucumis sativus	Asian cucumber	qing gua or huang gua	tseng kwa or wong gua	burpless cucumber, Chinese cucumber, long cucumber
Cucurbita maxima, *C. moschata*	Chinese pumpkin	nan gua	nam gua	Oriental pumpkins, Oriental squash, kabocha
Eleocharis dulcis	water chestnut	ma ti	ma tai	Chinese water chestnut
Glycine max	soybean	mao dou	wong dau	edamame (when green), da tou

(Botanical, English, and Chinese Names, *continued*)

Botanical Name	Common English Name	Mandarin Name	Cantonese Name	Alternate Common Names
Hemerocallis fulva	daylily	jin zhen cai	gum jum	tawny daylily, tiger lily
Luffa acutangula	luffa	ling jiao si gua	you lin si gua	ridged skin luffa, angled luffa, Chinese okra
Luffa cylindrical	luffa	tsee gwa	si gua	sponge luffa, smooth luffa, dishrag gourd, vegetable sponge
Momordica charantia	bitter melon	ku gua	foo gwa	bitter gourd, balsam pear, kerala
Nasturtium officinale	watercress	xi yang choy	sai yeung tsoi	
Nelumbo nucifera	Chinese lotus	lian ou	lin ngau	sacred lotus
Pisum sativum var. macrocarpon	snow pea	shid dou	ho lan dou	sugar pea, edible-podded pea
Psophocarpus tetragonolobus	asparagus pea	si jiao dou	sz kok dau	goa bean, winged bean, four-angled bean
Raphanus sativus	Chinese radish	loh bo	loh baak	daikon, Oriental radish
Sagittaria sagittifolia	arrowhead	ci gu	chee koo	Chinese arrowhead, swamp potato, kuwai
Sesamum indicum	sesame	zhi ma	chih ma	goma
Solanum melongena	Chinese eggplant	gie zi	ngai kwa	aubergine
Vicia faba	fava bean	can dou	tsaam dou	broad bean
Vigna angularis	adzuki bean	xiao hong dou	siu huhng dau	aduki bean, azuki, red bean
Vigna radiate	mung bean	lu dou	luhk dau	Chinese green bean
Vigna unguiculata ssp. sesquipedalis	yard-long bean	chang jiang dou	dau gok	asparagus bean, Chinese long bean
Zingiber officinale	ginger	jiang	geung	shoga

USDA Hardiness Zone Map

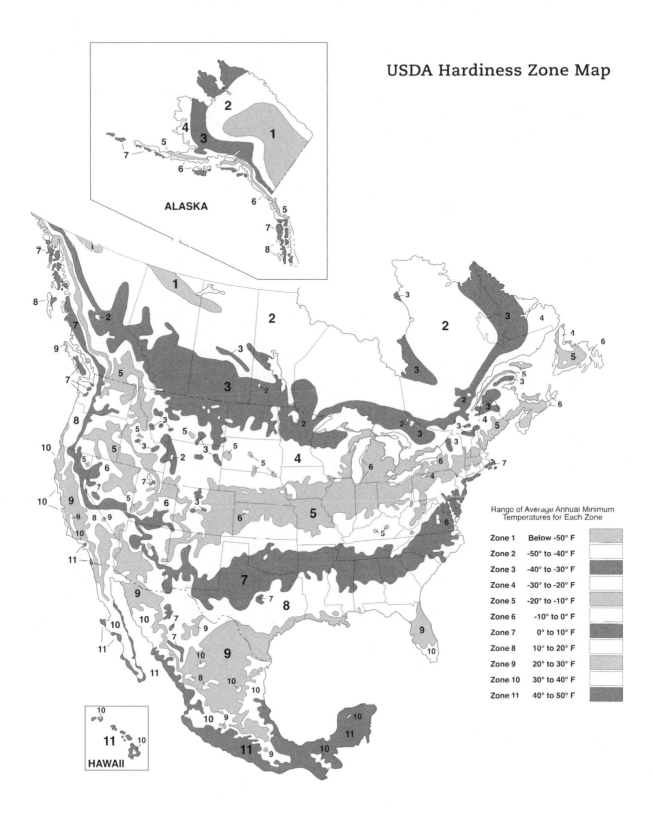

ALASKA

HAWAII

	Range of Average Annual Minimum Temperatures for Each Zone
Zone 1	Below -50° F
Zone 2	-50° to -40° F
Zone 3	-40° to -30° F
Zone 4	-30° to -20° F
Zone 5	-20° to -10° F
Zone 6	-10° to 0° F
Zone 7	0° to 10° F
Zone 8	10° to 20° F
Zone 9	20° to 30° F
Zone 10	30° to 40° F
Zone 11	40° to 50° F

207

Planting Guide for Vegetables Started from Seed

Vegetable	Seed Depth	Distance between Plants	Distance between Rows	Cool or Warm Season	Days to Maturity
amaranth, vegetable	¼"	½"	18"	cool	50–100
bean, adzuki	½"–1"	2"–3"	18"–30"	warm	120
bean, fava	1–1½"	4"–6"	18"–36"	cool	65–90
bean, mung	½"	6"–8"	24"	warm	90–120
bean, yard-long	½"–1"	4"	24"	warm	60–90
broccoli, Chinese	½"	1"	12"	cool	60–80
burdock	½"–1"	6"	20"	cool	45
cabbage, Chinese	½"	1"	18"–30"	cool	70–80
chrysanthemum, garland	¼"–½"	2"	18"	cool	25–60
cilantro	⅙"	½"	18"	warm	60
cucumber, Asian	½"–¾"	3"	48"	warm	60
eggplant, Chinese	¼"–½"	24"	36"	warm	60–75
garlic (cloves)	½"	6"	12"		6–8 mo.
garlic chives	½"	12"–14"	20"	cool	24–90
garlic, elephant (cloves)	1"	12"	24"	cool	180
gourd, fuzzy	1"	2"	36"	warm	75–85
kale, flowering	½"	8"–10"	16"	cool	55–75
luffa	1"	3"–6"	60"	warm	115
melon, bitter	1"	6"–8"	48"–60"	warm	60–75
melon, pickling	½"	4"	60"	warm	65

Vegetable	Seed Depth	Distance between Plants	Distance between Rows	Cool or Warm Season	Dates to Maturity
melon, sweet	1"	18"	60"	warm	115–130
melon, winter	1"	8"–10"	48"	warm	150
mitsuba	½"	2"	18"	cool	60
mizuna	½"	2"	18"	cool	30–60
mustard, Chinese	¼"	2"	12"–18"	cool	35–50
onion, bunching	½"	2"	18"	cool	65
pak choy	¼"	2"	18"	cool	35–50
pea, asparagus	½"	6"	18"	cool	50
pea, snow	½"–1"	n/a	6"	cool	50–85
pepper, hot	½"	2"–3"	24"–36"	warm	65–85
pumpkin, Chinese	1"	18"–36"	60"	warm	130
radish, Chinese	½"	2"	18"–30"	cool	60–80
sesame	½"	1"	36"	warm	30–45
soybean	1½"–2"	2"–5"	24"–30"	warm	75–115

METRIC CONVERSION CHART

When the measurement given is:	To convert it to:	Multiply it by:
inches	centimeters	2.54
feet	meters	0.305
mils	millimeters	0.254
square feet	square meters	0.093
ounces	grams	31.1
pounds	kilograms	0.373
tons	metric tons	0.907
gallons	liters	3.785
°F	°C	°F – 32 × 5/9

Sources for Chinese Vegetables

WATER GARDEN SUPPLIERS

Lilypons Water Gardens
800-999-5459
www.lilypons.com

LiveAquaria.com
715-361-9432
www.liveaquaria.com

Van Ness Water Gardens
800-205-2425
www.vnwg.com

William Tricker, Inc.
800-524-3492
www.tricker.com

ASIAN VEGETABLE SEED OR ROOT SUPPLIERS

AgroHaitai Ltd.
519-647-2280
www.agrohaitai.com

Artistic Gardens & Le Jardin
du Gourmet
802-748-1446
www.artisticgardens.com

Baker Creek Heirloom Seeds
417-924-8917
http://rareseeds.com

Burgess Seed & Plant Co.
309-662-7761
www.eburgess.com

Comstock, Ferre & Co.
800-733-3773
www.comstockferre.com

Dimension Trade Company
503-577-9382
www.newdimensionseed.com

Evergreen Y. H. Enterprises
eeseedsyh@aol.com
http://evergreenseeds.stores.
   yahoo.net

Gourmet Seed International
575-398-6111
www.gourmetseed.com

Gurney's Seed & Nursery
513-354-1491
http://gurneys.com

Harris Seeds
800-544-7938
www.harrisseeds.com

Henry Field's Seed & Nursery
513-354-1495
http://henryfields.com

J. L. Hudson, Seedsman
orders@JLHudsonSeeds.net
www.jlhudsonseeds.net

J. W. Jung Seed Co.
800-297-3123
www.jungseed.com

Johnny's Selected Seeds
877-564-6697
www.johnnyseeds.com

Kitazawa Seed Co.
510-595-1188
www.kitazawaseed.com

Mountain Gardens
828-675-5664
www.mountaingardensherbs.com

Nichols Garden Nursery
800-422-3985
www.nicholsgardennursery.com

Park Seed Company
800-213-0076
www.parkseed.com

Pinetree Garden Seeds
207-926-3400
www.superseeds.com

Redwood City Seed Co.
650-325-7333
www.ecoseeds.com

Stokes Seeds
800-396-9238
www.stokeseeds.com

Thompson & Morgan
800-274-7333
www.tmseeds.com

Turtle Tree Seed
888-516-7797
www.turtletreeseed.com

Vermont Bean Seed Co.
800-349-1071
www.vermontbean.com

W. Atlee Burpee & Co.
800-333-5808
www.burpee.com

Water & Sun Corp.
877-439-7394
http://watersuntogether.com

Index

Text in *italic* indicates an illustration; text in **bold** indicates a chart.

Image Credits

Front cover and interior illustrations by © Meilo So

How-to illustrations by Alison Kolesar

Back cover photography by © Martin Jacobs/FoodPix/jupiterimages (winter melon, fuzzy gourd), © Maximilian Stock Ltd./Anthony Blake Photo Library/photolibrary (Chinese radish), © Photos.com/jupiterimages (Chinese cabbage)

Photography credits, color insert

Page ix, top left: © Susan C. Bourgoin/FoodPix/jupiterimages, top right: © Graham Kirk/Anthony Blake Photo Library/photolibrary, bottom left: Derek Hall © Dorling Kindersley, bottom center: © Michael Grand/Stockfood, bottom right: © Martin Jacobs/FoodPix/jupiterimages

Page x, top left: © Dinodia/Stock Connection/jupiterimages, top right, bottom right: © Martin Jacobs/FoodPix/jupiterimages, middle left: © Fridhelm-StockFood Munich/StockFood, middle right: © Gerrit Buntrock/Anthony Blake Photo Library/photolibrary, bottom left: © Matthew Benoit/BigStockPhoto

Page xi, top left: © Kitazawa Seed Company/www.kitazawaseed.com (variety: Green Striped), top right: © Martin Jacobs/FoodPix/jupiterimages, middle left: © Crystal Cartier Photography/Brand X Pictures/jupiterimages, center: © Eising Food Photography/StockFood, middle right: © Pink/jupiterimages, bottom left: © Photodisc, bottom right: E. Jane Armstrong/FoodPix/jupiterimages

Page xii, top left and right: © Graham Kirk/Anthony Blake Photo Library/photolibrary, bottom left: © Solzberg Studios/StockFood, bottom right: © Photos.com/jupiterimages

Page xiii, top left: © Maximilian Stock Ltd./Anthony Blake Photo Library/photolibrary, top right: © Lew Robertson/Botanica/jupiterimages, middle right: © Kin Hang Norman Chan/stockxpert, bottom left: E. Jane Armstrong/Botanica/jupiterimages, bottom center: Christine M. Douglas, © Dorling Kindersley, bottom right: © Eising Food Photography/StockFood

Page xiv, top left: © stockxpert, middle left: © Elizabeth Watt/FoodPix/jupiterimages, bottom left: © Digital Archive Japan/DAJ/IPNStock, center: © Image Source/jupiterimages, right: © Graham Kirk/Anthony Blake Photo Library/photolibrary

Page xv, top left and right: © stockxpert, bottom left: Neil Fletcher and Matthew Ward, © Dorling Kindersley, bottom inset: Clive Streeter and Patrick McLeavy, © Dorling Kindersley, bottom right: © Comstock Images/jupiterimages

Page xvi, top left, bottom right: © Graham Kirk/Anthony Blake Photo Library/photolibrary, top right: © Teubner Foodfoto-StockFood Munich/StockFood, bottom left: © Martin Jacobs/FoodPix/jupiterimages